Food, Clothes and Shelter is a pioneering view of twentieth century industrial archaeology, which both breaks away from the idea that industrial archaeology only consists of relics of the eighteenth and nineteenth centuries, and shows how the twentieth century can be researched and recorded now. Kenneth Hudson has chosen to look at twentieth century industrial archaeology through three basic human needs – food, clothes and shelter. All of these have been profoundly affected by new processes, materials and technology. Food is taken to include growing, processing, packing and selling it, and so the author explores, for example, the archaeology of the potato crisp, breakfast cereals, Coca-Cola and the supermarket. The chapters on clothes include the development of synthetic fibres, washing machines and the dry-cleaning industry. Shelter deals with such things as council housing and high-rise flats, and also with domestic equipment such as vacuum cleaners and refrigerators and the replacement of wooden surfaces by those made of plastics.

The author feels strongly that industrial archaeology should concern itself as much with people as with objects and technology, and a good deal of his research is based on conversations and correspondence with the people who worked in the industries concerned, thus preserving valuable first-hand experiences of this century of momentous industrial change.

Kenneth Hudson taught at the University of Bristol from 1947–54, when he left to join the BBC as a producer and industrial correspondent. In 1966 he took up an appointment as Senior Lecturer at the University of Bath. Since 1971 he has worked as a consultant for UNESCO on museums, and spends the rest of his time writing books – including *Industrial Archaeology : A New Introduction* and *A Pocketbook for Industrial Archaeologists,* both published by John Baker – as well as lecturing and broadcasting, both at home and overseas. He has been a member of the jury of the Museum of the Year award since 1975, and in 1977 organised the European Museum of the Year award.

Food, Clothes and Shelter

KENNETH
HUDSON

John Baker
London

Food, Clothes and Shelter

Twentieth Century
Industrial Archaeology

First published 1978
John Baker (Publishers) Ltd
35 Bedford Row, London WC1R 4JH
© Kenneth Hudson 1978

ISBN 0 212 97021 6

Hudson, Kenneth
   Food, clothes and shelter.
   1. Technology – History – 20th century
   I. Title
   609'04   T19

   0-212-97021-6

Printed in Great Britain at
The Pitman Press, Bath

Contents

List of Illustrations

Introduction

During the past fifteen years, a considerable number of books has appeared, on both sides of the Atlantic, on what was once called 'the new subject of industrial archaeology'. The meaning of the term is now reasonably well understood – the systematic study of what remains of yesterday's industries and transport on the original site – but lately there has been considerable disagreement as to what industrial archaeology is for and what its limits should be. In the midst of the controversy, the present author can do no more than state his own opinion as clearly and unequivocally as possible.

Research must start with a model, which will say, in effect: 'This, on the basis of the best information available to us, is how we imagine the situation to have been. Goods were made, moved and sold in this way by these kinds of people. The physical and psychological atmosphere in which work was carried out seems to have been as follows. The business seems to have been profitable or unprofitable for these reasons. The new techniques which were being introduced at the time were this and that. The particular concern we are studying was quick or slow to take them up and apply them.'

We then proceed to use the archaeological evidence to test the model. If we construct no model to begin with, a great deal of our investigation is either irrelevant or wasted. Since we have not decided what questions we want answered, we are exploring the material in front of us in a desultory or disconnected manner and it is very likely, if not certain, that we shall overlook valuable clues as a result. The model need not, of course, cover the whole of the material available. Our specialist interest may, for instance, lie in reinforced concrete, works canteens or ventilation systems and in this case we shall be approaching our archaeological work with a model relating to this particular aspect of the industrial past. Or we may be wholly concerned with electric power, with synthetic fibres or with the construction of automobiles, so that a wide range of information relating to this particular industry will be used to build our original model.

Someone, however, has to work out what we might call a master model, to cover the industrial development of the period as a whole.

This is needed because there are overall trends and phenomena affecting industry as a whole, not individual sections of it. The micro-models and the archaeological work arising from them will, of course, contribute to the macro-model, but the development of both has to go on simultaneously, if the most fruitful results are to be obtained in the shortest possible time. There can and should be no real end to the process. The writing of history, of whatever branch, should be based on a series of models, which are discarded and replaced as their temporary usefulness is exhausted. If this is not done, history fossilises, mistakes are perpetuated and evidence lies mouldering and decaying for lack of use.

A great deal of the work carried out by industrial archaeologists during the past twenty years has to be written off, not so much as a failure, but as a false start, because it has not been based on models. For this reason, it has been almost purely descriptive or, to use a word which has recently become popular among the critics of industrial archaeology, antiquarian. It tests nothing, illuminates nothing, causes no revolution in thinking. This is not to say that archaeological description is useless or beside the point. In a situation such as we have been passing through in Britain since the end of the Second World War, where old buildings and machinery have been destroyed on an unprecedented scale, any kind of recording is better than none and some at least of the written descriptions, photographs and films which have been made during this period will be valuable to future historians who will, of course, have questions to ask which were not in the minds of the people who made the original observations and surveys. But, even in the atmosphere of urgency, sometimes desperate urgency, which has been familiar to industrial archaeologists during the past two decades, questions could and should have been asked which were not asked, time has been wasted because theory was inadequate and models were thought to be a fad or a luxury.

Until now most industrial archaeologists have been obsessed – the word is not too strong – with the eighteenth and nineteenth centuries, with the age of iron, steam and railways. Some of them have gone so far as to say that industrial archaeology, by definition and almost by Divine ordinance, is the archaeology of the Industrial Revolution. Such a parochial attitude is based on an interesting pattern of thinking, partly conscious, partly not. There seem to have been two fundamental reasons for this over-concentration on the earlier period of industrialisation. The first is that the eighteenth and most of the nineteenth century was the period of British industrial supremacy, the period when Britain taught the world its habits and techniques, exported widely and grew fat on the proceeds. In Britain's present miserable, down-at-heel state it is natural to want to look back and to draw patriotic comfort and encouragement from the days when things were different. There is every temptation to concentrate on the nineteenth century and avert one's gaze from the twentieth. The second reason for the Industrial Revolution fixation is that until the twentieth century industry was on a conveniently compact and simple scale. Machinery was not too big, it was relatively easy to understand, even for people with no technical training, and enthusiastic conservationists have been able to lead campaigns to save this or that memento of our industrial past with some hope of success. Georgian

The First Industrial Revolution – beams of the Cornish pumping engines over the shaft at Sudbrook, at the Welsh end of the Severn Tunnel. This picture was taken in 1966: the engines have now been demolished, despite great efforts to save them, and the work is now carried out by small electric pumps

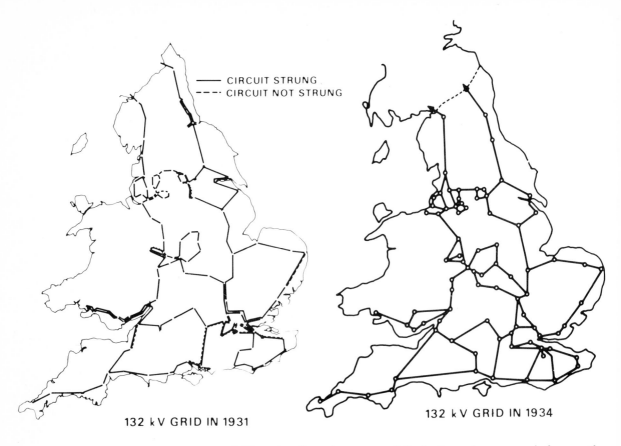

CIRCUIT STRUNG
CIRCUIT NOT STRUNG

132 kV GRID IN 1931

132 kV GRID IN 1934

and Victorian factories were solidly built and were not infrequently blessed with a romantic appearance and location, especially in the rural areas. The monuments of twentieth century industry, by contrast, are felt to be utilitarian, hardly old enough to be interesting and, worst of all, too large, in many instances, to make preservation a practical proposition. Technology, too, has been growing more complicated each year and the economic, social and architectural historians who still form most of the 'professional' backbone of industrial archaeology have tended to feel intolerably perplexed and humiliated when faced with the hardware and the theory of what one may perhaps be allowed to call the Second and Third Industrial Revolutions, that is, with the industries of the twentieth century. The division between First, Second and Third is by no means neat and tidy, but, broadly speaking, the First depended on steam, coal, iron and railways; the Second on petroleum, electricity, aluminium and aeroplanes; and the Third, which is still in its infancy, on electronics, plastics and man-made fibres. These three stages of industrial development contain a great deal of overlapping – one did not stop using railways once automobiles and aeroplanes were invented, or washing with soap once detergents arrived on the scene.

This, however, is a problem to be dealt with and overcome, not a reason for drawing a time line across industrial archaeology and saying

The Second Industrial Revolution – the creation of a national electricity supply system: (left) progress of the 132 kV grid, 1931–4; (above) stringing the grid – work in progress on the Little Barford/ Peterborough line showing temporary towers carrying conductors, 1936

that the subject officially ends in 1900 or 1914 or at some other arbitrary point. The real tasks confronting industrial archaeologists today are, in order of priority, to accept and welcome model-building and model-testing as the normal method of work, no matter what historical period is being dealt with; to come to grips with the special opportunities and difficulties of the twentieth century; and to rework, using models, what has been discovered about the archaeology of the First Industrial Revolution. Once this approach is being widely followed, industrial archaeology will be on the way to receiving what it has always longed for, the accolade of an academic discipline in its own right. It should go without saying, although in some circles the point still needs to be spelt out, that in constructing models one should use all the information at one's command, no matter to which specialist academic field it may belong. If one is aiming at a more complete, more satisfying historical understanding, there is no more virtue in being a 'pure industrial archaeologist' than a 'pure economic historian'. The industrial archaeologist will necessarily pay particular attention to the archaeology, because this is where his special skills and knowledge lie, but, if he is to make sense of archaeology, he must of necessity know a great deal about the general history of the period he is studying. Archaeology is only one of the historian's tools and no archaeologist

5

should be ashamed or frightened to think of himself as an historian first and as an archaeologist second.

The present book is a pioneering attempt to show how at least part of the industrial archaeology of the present century might be researched and written. The range of possible industries is, of course, very wide – far wider, one should emphasise, than the nineteenth century could offer – and, for practical reasons, a fairly drastic selection is inevitable. It has therefore been decided to concentrate on those groups of industries which cater for three of the basic human needs, Food, Clothes and Shelter. Since 1900, far-reaching changes of technology and organisation have taken place in all these fields, and it seemed useful to draw attention to them and to outline the kind of research which industrial archaeologists might be usefully carrying out, once the eighteenth and nineteenth century stranglehold has been broken and all fear of being considered a backdoor social historian has been banished.

The archaeologist who decides to busy himself with twentieth century material has one enormous advantage over the traditionalists. There are old men and women still alive who can tell him how things were in the early days of the industry which provided them with a living and to which they devoted their working lives. To be able to meet these people and to collect their reminiscences not only adds

Trafford Park, Manchester. The former Metropolitan Vickers factory, as it is today

6

another dimension to one's work, but provides the researcher with an opportunity to avoid the mistakes that are inevitably made by the person whose informants are all dead and who has to do the best he can with written material and with the survivals of buildings and machines. One may have taken great pains to locate and survey old machines and industrial premises and to discover, from records of all kinds, as much as one can about them, but the perspective changes and the interest grows when one is able to hear the workers' own version of what took place. Better still, a chance remark by one of these veterans often suggests a line of enquiry that would never have occurred to even the most lively-minded and imaginative specialist, left to his own devices.

The terms Food, Clothes and Shelter have been fairly liberally interpreted. Food is taken to include growing, processing, packing and selling it. All these aspects of feeding people have undergone profound changes during the present century and both the archaeology and the memories of the people directly concerned have been quite absurdly neglected. The present book is therefore concerned with such culturally significant food products as the potato crisp, the wrapped and sliced loaf, the milking-machine, the supermarket and Babycham. Under the heading of Clothes we shall consider such topics as the development of synthetic fibres, the introduction of washing machines, detergents and the growth of the dry-cleaning industry, and the rise and fall of the market for good quality mass-produced clothing. The two chapters devoted to Shelter will deal, among other points, with the beginnings of council housing, the design and production of prefabricated housing, the first high-rise flats, the early days of vacuum cleaners, Formica, refrigerators and of modern types of cooking equipment.

Research for the book has fallen into four parts:

(a) Discussion with industrial firms about the development of their own industry. This has included the use of the archives both of individual firms and of their trade associations.

(b) Visits to present and past premises of these firms, especially to get a proper idea of the change of scale and amenity which has taken place over the years.

(c) Visits to museums, to look at machinery and equipment which belongs to the past of an industry and which now survives only in museum collections.

(d) Conversations with past and present members of the staff of industrial organisations. These have been tape-recorded and the transcripts sent to the people concerned, for their comment. Often this unlocks further memories, which would have remained hidden and lost without the stimulus of reading what had originally been said. This face-to-face research has been supplemented by what has been gathered from another invaluable source, letters to local newspapers which ask for information from people who worked at a particular place or who have memories of a different kind relating to it. The remarkable results achieved in this way show how pleased people are to be invited to take part in a co-operative attempt to reconstruct the past and what a mass of useful detail exists, ripe for collection by anyone who is prepared to do it.

The photographs which illustrate the book come from a variety of sources. Some have been found in company and public archives, some in private collections, and some have been specially taken to show old industrial premises as they appear today.

The book has been written in the hope that many other people will become enthusiastic about the twentieth century as a field suitable for the industrial archaeologist's attentions and that, in this way, the notion that Britain's industrial importance died with Queen Victoria may be shown to be ill-founded. The author hopes he may be pardoned for holding and expressing the appallingly heretical belief that far too many old industrial buildings, mostly dating from the age of iron, coal and railways, are still standing and that the national morale would be greatly improved if nine-tenths of them were cleared away to make room for premises better suited to the modern industries by which we have to earn our living. But to demolish without proper recording is an act of social irresponsibility, comparable only with the ignorant and foolish destruction of company archives. The words 'ignorant and foolish' are carefully chosen. One of the saddest experiences one can have is to talk to big, successful companies which have prospered as a result of a long process of mergers, elimination of competitors and concentration on the immediate needs of survival, growth and profit-making and which are today trying to compile the history of the past 50 years, having thrown away the documents and photographs which are necessary to allow the job to be done properly. Organisations such as Tesco and Heinz would dearly like to have access now to the kind of records which they so cheerfully and confidently threw away during the 1940s and 1950s.

one Food: production and processing

One might say, as a generalisation, that any substance which fuels the human machine is entitled to be called food. The fact that some substances are more sought after than others is of considerable social importance. So, too, are the changes in food fashions and the ways in which these fashions can be influenced and manipulated by people with an interest in doing so. One recalls, for instance, that at the beginning of the present century the importers had a hard struggle to persuade the British public to eat bananas during the autumn and winter months, or to try the new American breakfast cereals at any time of the year. The archaeology of food in this century is consequently concerned with the early days of what one can fairly call completely new forms of food and drink – Babycham, Coca-Cola, potato crisps, Corn Flakes – with new ways of dealing with existing products – sliced and wrapped bread, tinned soup, fish fingers, frozen peas, pasteurised beer – and with new methods of producing raw materials – milking machines, tractors, artificial fertilisers. These are changes in commercial techniques, but we also have to reckon with the revolution that has taken place in the preparation and preservation of food on a domestic scale. Refrigerators, freezers, electric food mixers, toasters, have a history and archaeology of their own and an equal claim to be included in any consideration of food processing.

The social and economic background to the twentieth century food revolution – the term is not too strong – has involved both production and marketing. On the production side, there has been a continuous and successful effort to make the labour of each person employed in agriculture yield a higher output of food. This has meant, for the most part, applying American inventions to British conditions, but the investment in machinery has meant that the conditions themselves have had to be changed, in order to obtain a better return on capital. Working units have become steadily larger throughout the present century and production per acre higher, partly as a result of improved techniques, but even more through heavy expenditure on fertilisers and pesticides.

The revolution in the marketing of food has come about in a rather jerky fashion in order to meet such major social changes as the rise in

1920s advertisement for Coca-Cola from The Ladies Home Journal

working-class spending power – spectacular, by comparison with what was regarded as normal in Victorian times – with the increase in the proportion of working wives in all classes, with the ownership of domestic refrigerators and freezers and with a wish to spend less time on the more traditional kinds of housework. In the attempt to meet these new conditions, retailing, like farming, has become organised on a much larger scale.

In considering these changes it is logical to begin at the growing and rearing end of the chain. The extensive use of artificial fertilisers divides the twentieth century from the nineteenth. What was exceptional in 1850 had become widespread by 1900 and normal by 1950. The scale and profitability of the fertiliser industry both expanded enormously over this period. In the middle of last century, when most farmers were remarkably ignorant about chemical matters and when there was no worthwhile legislation to protect them against unscrupulous merchants, swindling was almost the rule. There was a great deal of adulteration of manures, no standard or compulsory form of description and little guidance as to what the constituents of fertilisers were or should be. 'If ever there was a time when the agriculturist had need to exercise especial caution in purchasing artificial manures', wrote Britain's leading agricultural chemist in 1855, 'that time is the present: for the practice of adulterating standard artificial fertilisers, such as guano, superphosphate of lime, nitrate of soda, etc., has reached an alarming point. . . . Some artificial manures are actually sold and bought at double or triple the price they are worth.'[1]

The situation steadily improved during the second half of the century, when the more successful of the merchants concerned came to understand that their reputation and their bank balance were closely connected. It is approximately true to say that until the First World War farmers continued to be supplied with fertilisers and seeds on a regional, if not a local basis, and the firms selling these commodities were consequently very widely scattered over the country and, by modern standards, small and primitive. The half-century following 1920 saw the development of two giants in the fertiliser business, Fisons and ICI, who between them absorbed nearly every one of the previously independent concerns. Production became concentrated at only a few centres, new factories were built and the old premises demolished or sold off for other industrial uses. As a result, the fertiliser industry offers the historian much better opportunities than the archaeologist, although, for those with the necessary time and patience, there can be some remarkable discoveries. One such is the circular building now forming the restaurant of the Dragonara Hotel, near St Mary Redcliffe Church in Bristol. This was originally a glass cone or kiln, built c. 1780 and the only one to survive from the many glassworks that were a feature of Bristol for more than two centuries.

[1] Dr Augustus Voelcker, *Journal of the Bath and West of England Society*, 1855, p. 62.

During the present century it was used for mixing chemical fertilisers, and in the late 1930s its top was removed, reducing the height from sixty to twenty-five feet. The opposite process, from hotel to fertilisers, can be seen at Felixstowe, where the handsome Felix Hotel was bought by Fisons in 1952, converted into their head office and renamed, in the industrial romantic style, Harvest House.

England was the birthplace of the superphosphate industry, and by 1870 there were about 80 factories making it, all at river or sea-ports, to which the imported phosphate rock could be easily brought direct by ship. Two of the companies concerned, Fisons and Packards, had factories at Bramford, in Suffolk, alongside the Ipswich–Stowmarket canal. The amalgamation of Fisons and Packards in 1919 was the foundation of the present company, which has 63 subsidiaries and employs more than 10,000 people. The archaeology of Fisons consequently falls into two parts – what survives of the premises of many companies which have been taken into the Group during more than 50 years and the buildings erected by the Group itself since its formation in 1919. The study of the sites of those factories which fall into the first category – those at Bramford, for instance, and Thetford – is important as a reminder of the very small scale on which business was being conducted even at the beginning of the twentieth century. In 1901 Packards' total sale of fertilisers was no more than 20,000 tons, only 5500 tons of which went to British farms. Production of this order required a works of extremely modest size and, equally important, very few ships to bring in the raw material. It was in every way a small-town industry, although, especially under the conditions of a century ago, the fumes and smell produced by treating phosphates with sulphuric acid and from the sulphuric acid plant itself made even a small fertiliser factory an unwelcome close neighbour.

With each new factory commissioned by the Fison group one can watch the scale of growth – and potential nuisance value – of fertiliser manufacturing. Cliff Quay, Ipswich – the first modern fertiliser factory on a deep water quay – began production in 1934 with an output of superphosphate of 80,000 tons a year. The need to safeguard supplies of ammonia, from which nearly all the nitrogen required for compound fertilisers was obtained, and which had hitherto come mostly from Germany, caused the building in 1937–9 of a large synthetic ammonia plant at Flixborough, near Scunthorpe. The extension of this plant during the 1950s and the introduction of new processes made it even more vulnerable to the kind of accidents which are almost bound to happen as a result of human error. Such an accident occurred in 1973 and caused not only great devastation in the locality, but disillusionment with the notion of growth and technical progress in the chemical industry. Progress from the little and comparatively harmless East Anglian factories of the 1840s, which dissolved crushed bones in acid, was complete. The size of Flixborough, viewed in conjunction with Fisons' fertiliser works at Avonmouth and their basic slag plant at Corby, illustrates in an

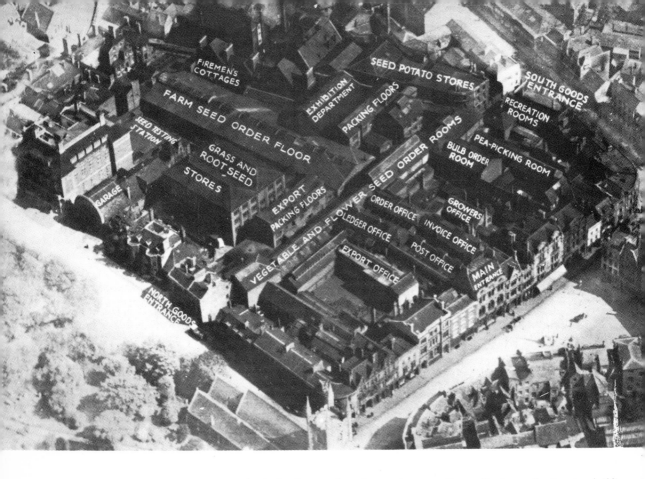

FIREMEN'S COTTAGES

SEED POTATO STORES

SOUTH GOODS ENTRANCE

EXHIBITION DEPARTMENT

PACKING FLOORS

RECREATION ROOMS

FARM SEED ORDER FLOOR

SEED TESTING STATION

GRASS AND ROOT SEED

SEED ORDER ROOMS

PEA-PICKING ROOM

STORES

BULB ORDER ROOM

EXPORT PACKING FLOORS

VEGETABLE AND FLOWER SEED ORDER ROOMS

GROWERS OFFICE

GARAGE

ORDER OFFICE

INVOICE OFFICE

LEDGER OFFICE

POST OFFICE

EXPORT OFFICE

MAIN ENTRANCE

NORTH GOODS ENTRANCE

Seeds for farms and gardens – Suttons Seeds, Reading. Aerial view of buildings (with buildings labelled) before demolition in 1960s

Suttons Seeds: new headquarters building, London Road, Reading. First occupied in 1960s, abandoned for environmental reasons in 1970s

unequalled way what a century of mergers and technical development has achieved in the fertiliser industry. These great inland chemical works are the foundations on which our agriculture now rests.

The same trend has been noticeable in the seed trade. In Victorian times it was normal for the same merchant to supply his local customers with fertilisers, animal feeding stuffs and seeds. Towards the end of the century, however, specialisation had become more marked and during the twentieth century the closing down of the smaller seed and feeding-stuffs firms has been very pronounced. It is interesting to examine the history of Britain's leading seed firm, Suttons, in this connexion. John Sutton established his business in Reading in 1806, dealing in corn and agricultural seeds. It prospered to such an extent that in 1858 it received the Royal Warrant. The interest shown in gardening by the Victorian upper and middle class caused Suttons to develop an extremely successful secondary business in flower and vegetable seeds. By the 1950s the offices, warehouses and packing sheds in the centre of Reading occupied more than five acres. By then the site had become extremely congested and, as real estate, very valuable. In 1962, therefore, the Royal Seed Establishment left its old home, having sold off most of the site to the Prudential Insurance Company, and moved to a new and splendid headquarters on the Trial Grounds, just outside the city. 'These modern buildings,' the Company announced, 'designed on contemporary lines, embody all the features necessary for the economic running of a great and important seed business. Without doubt these premises are the most up-to-date of their kind in the country.'

Fourteen years later Suttons left Reading and re-established themselves at Torquay. The 1962 building, our most distinguished example of twentieth century seeds-archaeology, is now used as a general office block, not by Suttons, and warehouses have been built on the Trial Grounds. What has happened to Suttons is in many ways typical of the twentieth century. A small Victorian business has grown into an international concern. The extension of the motorway network into Devon and the use of road, instead of rail transport for the company's goods makes location on a railway no longer necessary. The modern passion for image-building suggests rural Devon rather than suburban Reading as the best kind of site for a seed company. The further away from a strongly unionised area one can get, the better for one's peace of mind. From the patriarchal firm in the centre of Reading to the Queen's Award for Industry firm on the outskirts of the same town to the away-from-it-all firm at Torquay, Suttons have made a twentieth century industrial pilgrimage and, thanks to the miraculous survival of one of the old sheds under the windows of the Prudential, there is the archaeology to document it.

Nearly every farm is to some extent a site worthy of the attentions of the industrial archaeologist. A completely new set of buildings, severing all connexions with the past, is a rarity. Farmers are by nature thrifty people, who prefer to adapt a structure, instead of pulling it down, wherever possible, and for those with an eye trained to pick out the significant clues, a hundred years and more of agricultural history is to be picked out in any set of farm buildings. One can see the transition from horses to tractors, from steam to electricity, from hand to machine milking, from churns to tanks, from reaper-binders to combines, from poultry and pigs running about loose to poultry and pigs never stirring from an electrically lit, windowless unit. Agricultural buildings, like industrial buildings, demonstrate the widespread preference for systems and materials which are cheaper, lighter, more maintenance free and, eventually, easier to pull down and scrap than the masonry structures they have succeeded. A twentieth-century farm, like a twentieth-century factory, is an affair of steel, asbestos-cement and concrete, with little to be called picturesque about it.

On a farm one is looking at half of the agricultural industry, the other half being the people and places that manufacture agricultural equipment and supplies. A factory making tractors, ploughs and milking machines is as firmly a part of agriculture as a farm itself. The industry, and therefore its history and its archaeology have to be considered as a whole. This, however, is not to say that all parts of it have moved at the same pace or displayed the same attitudes. The American farmer, chronically short of labour since the days of the first settlement, has always been eager to try new machinery and methods, but in Britain farmers have taken a good deal of convincing that time is money. The very slow progress of the milking machine in this country is a case in point. In 1934, when milking machines were almost universal in the United States, Alfa-Laval sold only 265 in Britain. Forty years and a major war later, it would be difficult to discover a British farm where the cows are still milked by hand. During this period most British dairy farmers have changed their milking equipment at least once and in many instances three times, with the result that a milking machine installation of the 1940s is now a great rarity, either in a museum or on the farm.

One needs to remember, however, that, largely because of the reluctance of the British farming industry to invest in mechanisation, the pioneering factories making the new equipment, some of which trickled through to Britain, were overseas. The British market was not large enough to justify the expense and risk of manufacturing here. So, until well into the 1920s, Fordson tractors were imported from America and assembled at Ford's automobile plant at Trafford Park, Manchester. Other American manufacturers, such as Massey-Harris, did the same. The very few tractors which were made in Britain before the First World War were produced as a sideline by general engineering firms like Ruston and Hornsby at Lincoln. The two leading manufacturers of milking machines in Britain, Gascoigne's and Alfa-Laval, would have gone bankrupt very early if they had been so foolish as to pin all their hopes on the sales of dairy equipment. In the case of Alfa-Laval, their milking machines were in effect

Alfa-Laval marketed limited numbers of the Omega suspended units (under the name Amo Machine) during the First World War. This particular machine was in use on a farm in Oxfordshire until March 1930, having given 12–14 years service

subsidised by their brewery installations and by their industrial separators and evaporators. Gascoigne's kept solvent by selling silos and cowstalls, as they waited patiently for milking machine customers to arrive.

This amounts to saying that most of the archaeology relating to the first quarter of a century of certain kinds of agricultural equipment is not to be found in Britain at all. The buildings we have came comparatively late, but it is possible, even so, to use the premises which were occupied at different dates as a means of illustrating the growth of the company and of the market, which is one of the most valuable services industrial archaeology can perform. In the case of Gascoigne's, the original small offices in the Market Place in Reading, used in the days when they were manufacturing nothing and trying to sell American imports, have been demolished, but the house into which they moved in 1927, Lynford House, Castle Street, is still there. Three years later, needing more space, they were at a new address in Castle Street, now demolished, and in 1933 in a larger building, also in Castle Street, which still stands. By 1939 British farmers were at last beginning to become seriously interested in auto-recording milking stalls and the company felt able to build a completely new factory and office block on the outskirts of Reading, in Berkeley Road, where it has remained ever since, although it has bowed to the almost inevitable by becoming a member of a larger international group concerned with agricultural and industrial engineering and materials handling.

Convenience packaging – the lift-top can. Coca-Cola first introduced cans in the late 1950s

It's the real thing. Coke.

Coca-Cola's 1970s style of advertising

One has to be cautious before saying that any company or industry is totally destitute of archaeology. How old does a factory or a piece of equipment have to be before one can say that it has archaeological value? The number of firms which can be safely excluded from the archaeological canon at any given moment is certainly very small. In order to qualify for non-archaeological status, such a firm would probably have to be installed in premises not more than two or three years old and with no building it had previously occupied still standing. Such cases are extremely rare, and in all other instances one can find something instructive and historically significant about a firm's past and present location. Some instances are undoubtedly more rewarding than others. A Coca-Cola plant, for example – there are four in Britain – consists now, exactly as it has done for the past twenty-five years, of a simple building which is required to fulfil four functions – to remove all the individual characteristics of the local water; to mix the treated and standardised water with the Coca-Cola ingredients received in steel drums from the United States; to put the resulting liquid into cans and bottles; and to act as a distribution, sales and record-keeping centre. At some stage in the future – the date seems impossibly distant at the present moment – Coca-Cola will no longer be produced or drunk and a detailed, accurate record of one of these plants, in words and pictures, will provide social and dietary historians with invaluable material. The archaeology of Coca-Cola is, one might well say, now; and recording has to be carried out before it is too late.

The same would be true of another enormously popular and successful child of the twentieth century, Babycham. Owing everything to inspired advertising, Babycham was first marketed nationally in 1953 and has made a large fortune for the Showering family which had the genius to think of the idea. Technically, there is nothing remarkable or revolutionary about the product at all – a fermented mixture of pear juice and, it is rumoured, apple juice, sold very profitably in tiny bottles. The factory, constructed in stages during the 'fifties, 'sixties and 'seventies, occupies a large site at Shepton Mallet, in Somerset. Its creation has involved the demolition of a number of old buildings and the preservation of a former silk mill, which now forms part of the office block. A superannuated and spectacular viaduct of the long-closed Somerset and Dorset Railway belongs to the company and is used very effectively as a backdrop to the factory's delightful gardens. The Babycham archaeology therefore falls into three parts – a silk mill dating from the beginning of the last century; a railway viaduct, constructed in 1874; fruit mills, buildings for storing and fermenting fruit juice, a bottling plant, box-store, transport depot and offices, built at various dates between 1953 and 1974. Adaptation and modernisation is going on more or less all the time and the buildings put up in 1953 or 1960 would certainly not be designed quite like that now. The Babycham factory is, in fact, a continuous accretion of archaeology, a series of industrial and

The revolution in drink – detail from an advertisement in Woman, *December, 1971*

Babycham Stage Two – the word 'champagne' has disappeared, as a result of a legal action. Cosmopolitan, *June, 1976*

technical strata and, as such, as fascinating and informative as the site of Knossos or Verulamium. The fact that the strata are above the ground, rather than below it, is of no significance.

The archaeology of another notable twentieth century contribution to the human diet, potato crisps, is more complex. Potato crisps, most unreasonably neglected by historians and archaeologists, were a French invention and a British development. They were first made just before the First World War by a Frenchman called Cartier. By 1914 he had installed himself in England and had changed his name to Carter. His business was on a very small, almost domestic scale, and in 1919 it was bought up by Frank Smith, whose name and company dominated the potato crisp market for nearly 40 years. Smith started up in very small premises in Crown Yard, Cricklewood, behind the Crown public house, which is still there. His 'factory' was in fact little more than two sheds. It had a couple of open pans, in which the chips were fried, and two simple machines, one for each pan, to slice up the potatoes. Frank Smith and one or two of his friends put all the money they had into this business. It grew fast and by 1921 it had been transferred to a disused factory canteen in Somerton Road, Cricklewood. This had belonged to Handley Page, who had used it to feed their workers during the First World War. With the ending of the war, the factory became redundant and Smiths moved in as Handley Page's tenant. This building has now been pulled down. The first stage in the archaeology of potato crisps as an industry no longer exists.

In 1928 they built themselves a prominently sited new factory at Brentford, on the North Circular Road, and stayed there for nearly 40 years. The factory, which still stands, was the first to be built in a style which became identified with Smiths – modern, in a between-the-wars way, and vaguely reminding one of a cinema, the dream-palace of a successful self-made man. Smiths' policy was to have a number of these factories dotted about the country and to use each of them as a distribution centre, as well as a manufacturing plant. The system worked well enough under pre-war conditions, but afterwards it was to become one of the main reasons for the company's decline. Their principal post-war competitors, Walkers (1946) and Golden Wonder (1965), established themselves from the beginning on the basis of one or two large modern factories and a distribution system which used large trunker-lorries.

The pioneers of the potato crisp industry are now dead or retired, or close to retiring. One of the old-timers at Smiths, Rosie Weatherley, is a case in point. She went to work in the office of the new Brentford headquarters in 1928, straight from school at the age of 14. At that time, it was still very much a family concern, with three of the Smith brothers, Frank, John and Harvey, at the Brentford factory, and a fourth, Alfred, running the factory at Brighton. Her reminiscences, together with those of her contemporaries, form a unique record of the manufacturing methods and technical changes in the industry. Without them and the file of Smiths' house magazine the early

The architecture of potato crisps – Smiths headquarters on the North Circular Road, as it was in 1956. Built in the late 1920s, and sold in the mid-1960s

development of what has become one of Britain's major food industries would have remained undocumented, since no history of the company has ever been written.

Until the late 1940s, Miss Weatherley remembers, 'the crisps were all made in small copper pans, each holding six gallons of oil, so that each production unit was under the control of one girl'. Each pan had its own cutting unit, so that she judged for herself how many potatoes she had to cut into the pan to make the equivalent of about two tins of crisps, each tin holding 24 bags. These took about two minutes to fry and then she scooped them out with something that resembled a large butterfly net made of wire and put them up on a draining board at the side while she chucked the next fry into the pan. By the time that was ready, she shot her original fry down a chute into the packing room below.

'Those were the days when we made a really good crisp. After the war they changed over to a method of production where the frying unit was in the shape of an oblong canal, so that there was a continuous bath of oil, the cut crisps going in at one end and being extracted with a belt at the other. The oil was being propelled along the canal all the time, taking just enough time to cook the crisps by the time it came out the other end.

'Now they use American-type cookers, which are very large pieces of electronically-controlled equipment, and the type of crisp that's being cooked with it is entirely different. With the disappearance of the individual pan, and later of the Gas Board cooker, as we used to call it, the crinkle went out of the crisp and it became very much thinner and lighter in colour. The original crisp had a crinkle because it was cut with a knife that had a serrated edge.'

Crisps, in other words, are no longer what they were, but since no laboratory or museum has preserved a bag of 1930s crisps for posterity to study, we are dependent on veterans' memories for the facts. Given the clue, we can, of course, ask other members of Miss Weatherley's generation about the crinkle, the thickness and the colour, checking and cross-checking until we are reasonably sure that the information is reliable. Sadly, no piece of the old equipment has survived, either as a museum piece or in private hands.

It was a smelly job, and people who worked at the crisp factories were easily recognised, because the smell of the fat got into their hair. The factories made their presence felt in the neighbourhood, too. 'The smell', remembers Rosie Weatherley, 'was overpowering and you could meet it as you walked to work, because the wind carried it a long way.' Nowadays the problem is nothing like so serious, since the machines are covered and have powerful extractors.

Wages were very low. In the early 1930s, the fryers got a maximum of £1 9s. 6d. a week. The packers were on piece work, and had 1¾d. for packing a tray of 20 bags, not forgetting to put in the blue paper twist of salt. A lot of the labour at Brentford was local, but some came from as far away as Notting Hill, on an 8d. workman's return ticket, which, for a six-day week, made quite a big hole in a wage of £1 9s. 6d. The work was very seasonal, with a peak at Easter, a bigger peak at Whitsun and then the biggest peak of the year at August Bank Holiday.

The prosperity of the company became so great that in its heyday it owned the parish of Nocton, in Lincolnshire, which formed part of its great potato-growing estate. Smiths appointed the vicar of Nocton, but always consulted the Bishop of Lincoln in the matter. The estate remained in the possession of the company until 1975.

Frank Smith stayed on as Managing Director until well after the 1939–45 war. When he was 75 he handed over control to his son-in-law, Cyril Scott, who had been in the business for some time. At that time, Smiths were still *the* crisp in the country and serious competition was virtually non-existent. After 1945, however, a very large number of people used their Service gratuity to try to set up as manufacturers of potato crisps. The company still preserves a large album in which are fastened a collection of bags used by 572 separate companies which were making crisps between 1945 and 1955. Within a few years all these companies, operating much as Frank Smith had done in his early days, had disappeared, with the one significant exception of Walkers.

Smiths ran into trouble in the late 1950s, a typical case of the firm which failed to realise the social and economic changes which had been brought about by the War and which was blinded by its previous success. They were suffering from the familiar industrial sickness of

20

resting on their laurels. Their methods of production, distribution and potato storage were out-of-date and their machinery was obsolete. By the 1960s, their major competitors had modern plant and modern business methods. Smiths were failing to compete and in 1960 they were taken over by an American company, General Mills, which has concentrated on the production of snacks, rather than potato crisps. The Brentford factory, between Staples Corner and Hanger Lane, was given up and is now occupied by a cosmetics company, representing another major twentieth century growth industry, and Smiths are now more modestly housed on a trading estate at Kew.

The history of potato crisps is to a great extent the history of packaging materials. The old method was to pack them in a kind of waxed paper, known as Glassine. This was not air-tight, and until the introduction of film, instead of paper, in the early 1960s, the shelf-life of a packet of crisps was reckoned to be one day, after the bags were taken from the sealed tin. Public houses tried to extend the saleable life by putting the bags in a covered glass jar which stood on the bar, but this was not a satisfactory solution. Modern packaging, using plastic film, allows crisps to be kept in good condition for up to twelve weeks.

Crisps now appear to be passing into their third phase of development. After first losing their crinkle, they are now beginning to be made, not from sliced potatoes, but from potato flour, a change which is guaranteed to make every crisp exactly like its fellows, with none of the little individual marks that chips straight from the potato always have. They have moved a long way from the situation outlined in a 1931 advertisement in the *Daily Telegraph*. 'No hiker's outfit', it said, 'is complete without Smiths Potato Crisps and nuts and seedless raisins. Obtainable in 2d. and 3d. packets from ham and beef shops, grocery and provision stores and village inns, etc.' Crisps are no longer mere picnic fare. They have become an item of everyday diet, a convenience food, and one of great commercial importance.

The Smiths story is important to the industrial historian and archaeologist in several ways, illustrating both a method of procedure and the nature and significance of the archaeological evidence relating to a twentieth century industry. Here, as with Morris Motors or with rayon, is an enterprise which started with an idea and very little capital in a back-street workshop and developed within ten years into a concern and a brand name known to most people in Britain. The speed of growth and the shortage of money during the formative years meant adapting any reasonably suitable building to one's immediate needs and abandoning it as soon as it had become impossibly small. The British-owned section of the motor industry has never been able to cut free from its early days and to establish itself in completely new buildings on a fresh site and its efficiency has greatly suffered as a result. Potato crisps, however, like much of the food industry, have done much better for themselves, mainly, perhaps, because a ramshackle, linked-to-the-past image is bad for any company whose business is food and drink, and for which the public face must suggest

The American-style food factory comes to London, complete with gardens and trees – Harlesden factory of the H J Heinz Company opened 1925. The author once worked behind the seventh window from the right on the top floor, in the front of the building

Interior of H J Heinz factory, Harlesden, c. 1930. The home-bottling atmosphere is very typical of the period

cleanliness, light and air. The factories erected by Frank Smith, looked at in their historical context, were intended to convey to the world the pride of a successful self-made man in a company which had arrived, and which occupied a monopoly position in its industry and to show that, manufactured in this kind of building on a dozen sites scattered over Britain, potato crisps were in the first league of modern, hygienically produced foodstuffs. To understand this properly, one has to remember that when the factories at Brentford, Bristol and elsewhere were built in the 'twenties and 'thirties the area surrounding them was not at all like it is today. In the case of the headquarters at Brentford, for instance, the North Circular Road before the Second World War was a prestige and comparatively pleasant highway, with an easy flow of traffic and a feeling of being, if not exactly on the edge of the country, within a short distance of it. Firms like Smiths which built new factories along the North Circular and Great West Roads were doing the fashionable thing.

The recipe for a food factory in the days when an inner city location meant dirt and congestion was grass, trees, space and air fit to breathe. Heinz miraculously achieved something surprisingly close to this in their factory at Harlesden, built in 1922, within the inner suburban limits, and Wrigley's did surprisingly well with a new railside factory at North Wembley (1928), abandoned in 1970 in favour of Plymouth and still, although empty, looking considerably younger than its years. The concept of the new-style food factory was imported into Britain from the United States, where the pioneers had been Gail Borden in dairying; H. J. Heinz in general food processing and William K. Kellogg with breakfast cereals. Their factories set an altogether new standard in hygiene and in pleasant working conditions for employees. Only when the Americans had set up manufacturing plants in Britain, a feature of the first quarter of the twentieth century, did the British companies begin to understand that a new age had dawned and that the old, grim, smoky, dockside environment which had previously been accepted as normal was no longer acceptable for any kind of foodstuffs with a strong consumer appeal. The Ovaltine factory, established in rural Hertfordshire by the side of the main railway line between Watford and Berkhamstead in the 1920s, with its own large poultry farm, was a symbol of the new trend.

In setting the new trend, the Americans had many years start over the British. Borden was building his milk processing plants in the 1860s, Heinz established his business in 1875, Kellogg founded the Battle Creek Toasted Corn Flake Company in 1906. The twentieth century success of proprietary breakfast cereals, to which the British were late converts, represents something very close to a manufacturer's dream – sealed packets largely filled with air – but its achievement has been made possible only as a result of great ingenuity, with remarkable processing developments for flaking, rolling, shredding, puffing, baking, grinding and re-vitaminising the simple grain to yield products of varying flavours, form and texture. No branch of twentieth-century manufacturing has owed more to advertising. The British had to be persuaded to adopt an American habit, which for many years they viewed with the greatest suspicion.

The classic example of a cereal manufacturer going for clean countryside conditions in Britain is Shredded Wheat, which has been in production at Welwyn Garden City for more than half a century. The Shredded Wheat Company was started in Canada at the end of last century by Henry Perky, an American lawyer. In 1908 the company began to export to Britain, with a sales headquarters at the Aldwych in London. Demand gradually built up and by the early 'twenties it had become obvious that a factory would have to be established in Britain. At that time Welwyn Garden City was in its infancy, dedicated to the ideal of having homes, places of work and open spaces in close proximity. Shredded Wheat found Welwyn attractive and opened a factory there in 1926, surrounded by green fields. Since then, history has caught up with it in two ways. In 1928 the company was taken over by the American National Biscuit Company, Nabisco, who claim to be the largest bakers in the world, and during its fifty years at Welwyn the factory has become surrounded by other industrial enterprises. It is no longer in the green fields, although the surroundings are still perfectly pleasant and seemly and the trees have grown considerably. One should try to imagine it, however, in the pioneering context of 1926, when there was a pure-food-produced-in-ideal-conditions crusade still to be preached.

Kelloggs, who began manufacturing much later in Britain, in 1938, developed their business very rapidly. Previously everything had been imported from Canada, sales in this country beginning in 1924. For a few years, only Corn Flakes and All-Bran were sold here, but when Rice Krispies were added to the range in 1928 the importing method became too clumsy and expensive. In 1938, after a period of experiment and temporary arrangements, the present factory at Stretford, on the Trafford Park Trading Estate, Manchester, was built. It has more than trebled in size since then and now produces more than a million packets of breakfast cereals a day, of 13 different types. Given a five-day working week and a factory operating for 50 weeks, this amounts to an annual production of 250 million packets, or about five packets for every man, woman and child in Britain. Since Kelloggs are not the only company making packaged cereals, the industry, which so far as Britain is concerned is entirely a twentieth century creation, is obviously an industry of considerable importance.

The siting of the Kellogg factory is significant. It was chosen primarily because of its suitability for handling imported raw materials, and for its open, waterfront location looking across towards the countryside. A link with the Bridgewater Canal provided a water route to Liverpool docks and a rail siding allowed finished products to be distributed all over the country. The Trafford Park Estate was established on this basis. Begun in 1896, it was essentially a canal and

The American-style food factory in hygienic rural surroundings – THE HOME OF SHREDDED WHEAT, Welwyn Garden City, 1926

railway estate, with exceptionally good facilities for the period. On one side there was the Manchester Ship Canal and on the other the Bridgewater Canal link. Railways for freight and trams for the workers completed the transport network. Since 1974, however, when their new grain terminal was built at Seaforth Docks, Liverpool, Kelloggs operate in a different way. The system of transporting grain by barge to Stretford has been replaced by road tankers, a procedure greatly helped by the new motorway link between Liverpool and Manchester.

All this amounts to saying that the earliest archaeology for Kelloggs in Britain goes back to 1938. The difference between the size of the plant in that year and today is a measure of the enormous growth of the packaged cereal industry during the past 40 years. Our one native company in this field, Weetabix, at Burton Latimer, Leicestershire, shows a similar pattern of growth. Beginning in the 1930s in an old flour mill, which still forms part of the factory complex, it has expanded into a modern plant six times the original size, a fact made clear in an aerial photograph.

In considering the twentieth century development of the food industries, one has to distinguish between, on the one hand, the 'old' or primary industries – sugar refining, flour milling, meat storage and wholesaling, fish processing and distribution – which have for the most part been willing or compelled to stay close to the docks and the

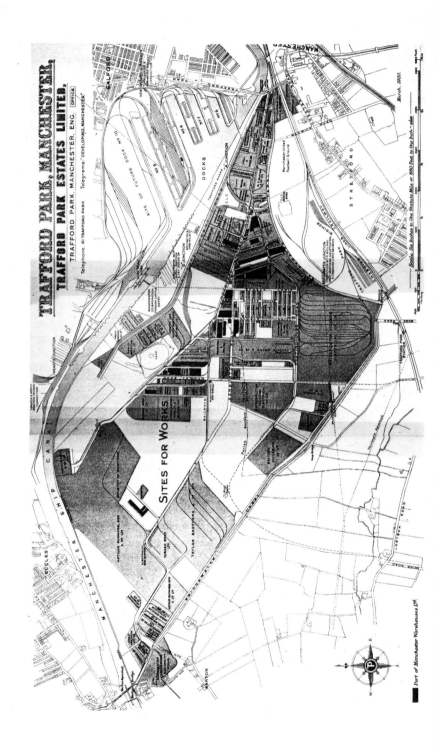

TRAFFORD PARK, MANCHESTER,
TRAFFORD PARK ESTATES LIMITED.

TRAFFORD PARK, MANCHESTER, ENG. OFFICE

Telephone 61 TRAFFORD PARK   Telegrams "DEVELOPING, MANCHESTER"

March, 1920.

Scale: Six Inches to One Statute Mile or 880 Feet to One Inch — or.

SITES FOR WORKS

■ Port of Manchester Warehouses Ltd.

railways, and on the other, the 'new', secondary food industries – canning and freezing plants, potato crisp factories, biscuit and chocolate factories – which for one reason or another find it advantageous to establish or re-establish themselves in more spacious and pleasant surroundings.

The frozen food industry belongs not merely to the twentieth century, but to the second half of the twentieth century. In 1977 it was estimated that the British retail and catering sales of frozen foods amounted to well over £400 million. In 1945 the trade did not exist. These figures do not include poultry and ice cream which, taken together, would add at least another £200 million to the total. Frozen foods had their origins in the United States, the most important pioneer being the splendidly named Clarence Birdseye, who set up his first fish freezing plant in New York in 1923. In 1924 he built his first automatic quick freezing machine and in 1940, when the United States entered the Second World War, frozen food sales there had risen to $150 million a year. By the time the war ended, many canners, meat packers, fish merchants, trawler owners and food distributors in Britain had become increasingly alive to the commercial possibilities of quick freezing. Much of the immediate post-war period production was concerned with fish and peas. This meant that the industry inevitably grew up at large fishing ports and in centres close to agricultural areas. Grimsby met both requirements and so did Lowestoft and Yarmouth. The Birds' Eye plant at Kirkby, nine miles outside Liverpool, has a more complicated history. On the Kirkby industrial estate there were, in 1952, buildings which had served as a munitions factory during the war and later as a mattress factory. Converted for the production of frozen foods, this factory was able to draw very conveniently on Lancashire farms for its supplies. The terms 'frozen' and 'quick frozen' are often used interchangeably, but they conceal important differences in respect of technology. 'Quick frozen' means that the food has been reduced rapidly by one of a number of processes to a temperature of $-18°C$, or below, and maintained at this temperature until it is sold to the customer who intends to cook and eat it. 'Quick frozen' foods should be distinguished from 'deep frozen' or 'frozen' foods, which are frozen slowly by conventional refrigeration methods, and from 'chilled' products, such as meat, which have been brought down to a temperature no lower than $0°C$. A variety of techniques has been developed to suit different types of foodstuff, but whichever method is used, the cost of quick freezing is inevitably high, which means that whatever is frozen must be of high quality, in order to sell for a good price and absorb the overheads. In order to achieve this, the processing firm must have the closest possible control over the raw materials coming into its factory. In the case of vegetables, this involves telling the growers what seed to use, supervising their methods of cultivation and making sure that the crop is harvested at exactly the right moment.

It would be no exaggeration to say that during the past 50 years the

Trafford Park, Manchester, the cradle of the Second Industrial Revolution. Plan showing site layout and location of different factories, 1911

Carreras factory, Mornington Crescent, London in the late 1930s. This factory, with its exuberant Egyptian-style façade, was the home of Black Cat cigarettes – two black cats can in fact be seen mounting guard in front of the main entrance. Food, drink and tobacco are usually classified together in Government statistics of employment and production, and there are those people – understandably popular with the industry – to whom smoking is more important than eating. A major change since 1939, and almost a social revolution in itself, has been the extension of the smoking habit to women. At the time when this factory was built, smoking was almost entirely a male pursuit

demands of the processers have brought about a revolution in British agriculture or horticulture entirely comparable with the changes which took place as a result of the much-quoted Agricultural Revolution of the eighteenth century. British farmers, or at least those of them who supply the canners, freezers and crisp makers, are no longer their own masters. If they are growing potatoes to be converted into crisps, the main-crop variety they have to grow is Record, which has a regular shape and even size and is not too large. If, however, they intend to sell potatoes for chip making, the larger the potato, the more favoured it is. The control over the grower can, for certain commodities, extend a long way beyond the frontiers of Britain itself. Baked beans are a good example. In proportion to its population, the United Kingdom is, for some reason, the world's biggest consumer of baked beans – every household buys, on average, one tin a week – with sales growing at the rate of 5% a year. The beans come mainly from Michigan and Ontario, but to a certain extent from Chile, Romania and Africa; the tomato concentrate from Portugal, with lesser quantities from Greece and Turkey. The quality of these supplies is rigorously controlled by the canners, who lay down specifications to which the growers and shippers must adhere.

The modern poultry industry would be unrecognisable to anyone who was producing eggs and chickens 30 years ago and who returned to the scene now after a long absence. Intensive methods began to be introduced in about 1953 and the industry now represents 14% of the British gross agricultural product, second only to dairy farming in size and importance. The day of the small firm is long past. The industry is now controlled by large, fully-integrated concerns, with their own specialist organisations for breeding, incubating, rearing, processing and marketing. Laying birds spend their whole productive life of 52 weeks in individual cages and during that time they are expected to lay 235 eggs. In their 53rd week after beginning to lay, they are slaughtered. The huge houses in which these birds live provide a fully-controlled environment, and are often equipped with automatic watering, feeding and, in some cases, automatic egg collection. Birds intended for the table run free on the ground in purpose-built houses of up to 30,000 capacity. It is not uncommon to find 250,000 or more table birds on a single farm at any given time.

The archaeology of food production and food processing falls into two categories. On the one hand, there are the premises which history has left behind – the surviving and long-abandoned buildings of the once-famous Ovaltine egg-farm by the side of the railway line near Hemel Hempstead, where hens could once be seen running happily around on the grass; the sheds, in which 20 or 30 cows – each with her own name and stall – used to stand quietly munching or being milked, and which are now used for storing bags of fertiliser and feeding-stuffs. In the second group are the early examples of buildings and structures which belong to the new technologies – Heinz at Harlesden, Bird's Eye at Great Yarmouth, Smiths on the North Circular Road, steel tower silos and wooden broiler houses dotted over the rural areas. In some instances, such as the original Weetabix factory mentioned above, the archaeology is twofold: the death of one food industry and the birth of another is commemorated in the same building. A very good example of this can be found at Wiveliscombe, in Somerset, where the very handsome Victorian brewery of Arnold and Hancock was sold, gutted and converted to the production of broiler chickens.

One can hardly leave a survey of the major twentieth century changes in the food and drink industries without some mention of the now huge petfood industry in Britain. It is estimated[2] that in 1975 half the households in the United Kingdom owned a pet of some kind. The peak may have been passed, since there was a 4% decline in ownership from 1973. There were 5.3 million dogs, 4.6 million cats and 2.5 million budgerigars. The average dog owner spent 155.7 pence a week on food for his pet, the average cat owner 98.6 pence. More significantly for the industry concerned with these matters, 62.5 pence

[2] *Pets and the British* Pedigree Petfoods, 1977.

in the case of dogs and 61.8 pence for cats went on canned petfood, which amounts to a very large market indeed. During the past 30 years, the manufacture of petfood has been one of the fastest growing industries in Britain. Whether or not it is about to enter a decline, as some predict, remains to be seen.

Ready-to-eat petfoods have become popular and perhaps inevitable at the same time as ready-to-cook human foods. Britain lives increasingly on ready-prepared dishes and on snacks, which contain no waste and therefore no scraps for the dog or cat. There are many households nowadays into which no meat bones and no fish other than fish fingers ever go. The beginning of the end of the old scraps, bones, offal and biscuit method of feeding dogs and cats was signalled in 1934 when the American confectionery manufacturer, Forrest E. Mars, bought a small Manchester company, Chappel Brothers, which canned poor-quality meat and sold it as petfood, under the brand name of Chappie. Mars transferred production of Chappie to the Slough Trading Estate. A cat food, Kit-E-Kat, was added to the range and by 1939 the annual turnover of the business had risen to a very modest £100,000. The original factory at Slough still stands, although Mars no longer has any connexion with it, and it is entitled to be called the birthplace of the modern petfood industry in Britain.

After the war, the business began to boom. By 1951 sales had reached £1 million and a move to a new site had become essential. Chappie consequently moved to an old textile mill at Melton Mowbray, recently vacated by Paton and Baldwins. It was a very small-scale operation. The old mill machinery had to be taken out and the machinery required for preparing and cooking petfood put in. Forty ex-Paton and Baldwin women and girls were taken on, 'very competent, cheerful, willing people', to work on the packing line. Sales rose fast, new buildings were erected and in 1953 the factory went over to continuous shift working. In 1957 Chappie Limited became Petfood Limited, and in 1974 Pedigree Petfoods. A second factory at Peterborough opened in 1974 and now the company, with sales of £100 million a year, is much the largest manufacturer of petfoods in Britain. As its raw material, it relies on what it diplomatically refers to as 'protein that is to a considerable degree a by-product of the human food industry'. In more exact terms, this means slaughterhouse offal and what remains of fish after the filleters have finished with it. Everything arrives in the form of huge, hard-frozen blocks, moved in and out of the cold-store like slabs of concrete. Herrings, once an important petfood ingredient, are now almost unobtainable as a result of fishing restrictions.

A visitor to one of the Petfood plants is likely to experience two reactions. One, and probably the first, is their size. The second is the up-to-date nature of the technology and the great care which is devoted to hygiene. There would be no problem in converting these factories at any time to the production of foodstuffs intended for human consumption. Most significant, perhaps, to anyone who is interested in the study of industries in their environment – a most important aspect of industrial archaeology – is the way in which this large factory complex has established itself in an area which had no previous experience of anything on a similar scale and where there was considerable suspicion and hostility to overcome. Melton had always been an agricultural town and a market centre, and local people, on the whole, liked it the way it was. 'They didn't,' recalled one of Pedigree Petfood's veteran employees,[3] 'like the thought of an animal petfood factory here. They thought of horrible smells. I heard of rumours, and they were believed by some people, that there would be herds of horses driven down the streets to be slaughtered, all these sorts of things.'

The emotion gradually died down and the fears disappeared and it is now possible for the firm to say, with complete justification, that over the past quarter of a century: 'We have brought prosperity to this town, and when you bring prosperity to a town it attracts other things. The local community would like other industries to come here and so would we. We don't like being as dominant as we are in this town. It's not good.'

The growth of the factory at Melton Mowbray, the firm's archaeology, has to be seen against this human and community background, to reveal the problems and achievements involved when a town is brought sharply face to face with the Second Industrial Revolution, after missing the First. The situation is not at all uncommon in rural areas and it will probably take another 25 years at least before what has happened can be seen in proportion. By that time, it is quite possible that the manufacture of dog and cat food will have departed from Melton and that some totally different industry will be installed in these premises. No harm will necessarily result from the change and the permanent benefit conferred by Pedigree Petfoods on the area may turn out to be that it has accustomed two generations of people to the realities and opportunities of factory work. This has already happened in many other places. At Cinderford, in the Forest of Dean, for instance, Meredith and Drew provided much-needed jobs in this old mining area, when they built a new biscuit factory in 1958. Ten years later they were absorbed by Associated Biscuits and the factory closed down. The site was taken over by an American concern, Engelhard Industries, who are in the very different business of refining and recovering precious metals, and who have since greatly extended the plant. But it was the biscuit factory which trained Cinderford's first industrial workers and established modern light industry in the area, and metal refining which reaps the benefit. If an industrial tradition had not already been established by the first firm, it is doubtful if the second would have been attracted to the area. Industrialisation is a cumulative process.

[3] Michael Brooshooft, 3rd December 1976.

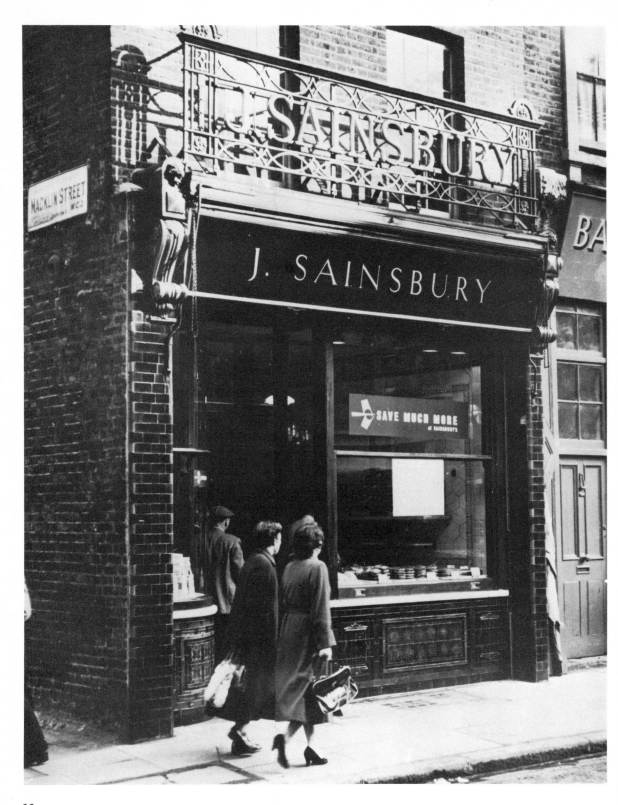

32

two Food: packaging and retailing

The story of food retailing can be told in general terms or as it affected individual firms. Both approaches are useful and both illustrate two unmistakable trends. The first is the creation of large retailing groups and of chains of shops; the second is characterised by the growth of the self-service system, and by the adoption of packaging for every category of goods. The two trends are closely connected. Without reliable packaging materials, self-service could not have developed, and without large groups, able to experiment and to risk considerable investment, self-service could hardly have come into existence.

The complete revolution in selling food to the public is illustrated by the history of Sainsburys. John Sainsbury opened his first shop at 173 Drury Lane in 1870. It sold dairy produce and it continued to operate, as part of the Sainsbury business, until the early 1970s, when it was demolished, together with the next door building, to make room, ironically, for a larger self-service shop run by a rival company. One can see from a photograph, however, how small the shop must have been, not more than fifteen feet wide, and with two floors and an attic over the shop.

By 1876, the Sainsbury business was expanding into branches. The first was at 159 Queen's Crescent, Somers Town, and the second, close to it and also in Queen's Crescent, two years later. The 1878 branch continued trading until 1968. At some time about 1880 Sainsbury planned a different kind of shop, which became the pattern for the firm's suburban stores for more than 70 years. There seems nothing particularly remarkable about it now, but it was a great novelty at the time, designed to be kept very clean, in an age not celebrated for cleanliness in the food trade. The floor, walls and counter-fronts were tiled and the counter-tops were made of marble. The shop front was elaborate, with the name 'Sainsbury' in gilded glass within a wrought iron frame. Inside, there were shelves and a continuous working area behind the assistants at the counters on either side of a central passage-way, which was reckoned to be wide enough to allow a pram to be pushed in comfort down the whole length of the shop. The first new-type Sainsbury shop, opened in Croydon in 1882, had the additional amenity of chairs for customers to sit on. Many subsequent branches

Sainsbury. The early narrow-fronted type of provision shop, in Drury Lane, shortly before its demolition in the late 1960s

33

were built in this style. Two of them, at 87 Balham High Road and 292 Kilburn High Road remained much the same until they were closed in 1969.

In 1914 Sainsburys had 115 branches. The previous 30 years had seen a spectacular growth by some of the food multiples. Thomas Lipton opened his first shop in Glasgow in 1871 and by 1899 he had 500. The Home and Colonial built up from nothing in 1885 to 400 shops in 1900. A mere statement of a number of branches is misleading, however, since many branches were very small and sold an extremely restricted range of foods. Sainsburys were no exception to the rule, some of their shops, such as those in Kensington and Hove, being much grander than the average.

In the early 'twenties most groceries were still being weighed and packaged from bulk at the counter. One could, however, see the beginnings of a new system. Assistants had always been expected to keep themselves occupied when trade was slack by weighing up and packing groceries to speed up service during the busy periods, and soon after the end of the First World War Sainsburys took the next logical step of having their bulk goods packed centrally at their warehouse in Blackfriars, using factory methods. Every opportunity was taken to enlarge the shops and by the 1930s most of them were organised on a six department basis – Groceries; Dairy Products; Bacon and Hams; Cooked Meats; Fresh Meat; Poultry and Game. Only the first two of these made use of prepackaging to any degree; the remainder required skilled counter staff for many years.

It is perhaps worth pointing out that until the 1930s the distribution of goods to Sainsburys' branches was carried out by horse van and goods train. The last of the horses and vans were not given up until 1937.

The United States began to use a rudimentary kind of self-service during the depression years of the 1930s. The method was neither scientific nor elegant. Cases of goods were simply placed, opened, on the floor of warehouses, customers took what they wanted and paid at the exit. A more sophisticated system, with shelves and check-out points, was developed during the war and the years immediately following and in the late forties the British Ministry of Food granted a small number of firms building licences, so that they could experiment with self-service methods. Sainsburys decided to use the branch at 9–11 London Road, Croydon – the first 'model' shop, opened in 1882 – as their guinea pig. Within the history of the firm, this building is consequently historic twice over. It was in every way experimental, and it began, in 1950, under great difficulties, since butter, bacon, cheese and fresh meat were all rationed – bacon and meat remained so until 1954 – and could not be sold on a self-service basis. The planners and engineers who made the early supermarkets worked out the design of the equipment as they went along, culminating in the building in 1953 in Lewisham High Street of what was at that time the biggest food supermarket in Europe, with a shopping area of 7500 square feet.

'I'm sure that housewives generally are becoming
very much more hygiene conscious, and in a self-
service shop, of course, it is absolutely essential that everything is wrapped and wrapped thoroughly and properly, and this does add to the
hygenic aspect of the food trading in this
fashion.
    'We do insist that customers take a wire
basket on coming into the store, to put their
purchases in. They're not obliged to put anything in them. They can walk out of the shop
without buying anything. Not everybody likes
having to use a wire basket. The other complaint, if it is a complaint, is that this form
of shopping perhaps makes the customer spend a
little more than she intended.
    'I think there will always be room for the
individual grocer in the small areas. But in
the main areas I think self-service of this
kind has got a big future, not only in the grocery and provision trade, but also in the
greengrocery trade as well.'

Mr Woods of Sainsbury, in a BBC radio broadcast 29.2.56

The new style Sainsbury, showing the size of site required

35

It so happens that Sainsburys have an unusually good photographic archive, so that the evolution of their shops can be studied, if not from the beginning, at least for most of the firm's history. One limitation is that until recently all the photographs are in black and white, which cannot do full justice to the atmosphere and appearance of any shop, especially a food shop, but with most retailing so poorly documented on the visual side, we should be grateful for at least one collection which offers such a continuous record, the result of unbroken family ownership of the business over more than a century.

The requirements for really satisfactory research into the history of any retailing concern are easy to state and difficult to fulfil. We need, ideally, reasonably full details of investment, trading and policy at different periods; a plentiful supply of photographs, advertisements and correspondence with suppliers; archaeological evidence, including old shop-fittings; the reminiscences of management, staff and customers; and, to move into what can unfortunately be only a dream world, samples of the goods sold decade by decade. In practice, we usually have to settle for something much less than this, which is another way of saying that to recreate the feeling, sound and smells of a food shop of 50 or 100 years ago is an artistic feat of the first order. No one who has not actually experienced it can have any real idea, for instance, of the wonderful range of smells which an old-fashioned grocer's shop offered, in the days when most goods were there ready for sale in sacks and boxes, hanging from the ceiling and open to the air, and no doubt to germs as well, on counters and marble slabs. Universal packaging and the self-service store have removed most of the old-fashioned sensory experiences from food shopping, which, to those who knew it, is a great deprivation. Because the evidence no longer exists, some things can no longer be proved. One can only say that in pre-war days eggs had thicker shells and bread tasted better, and hope to be believed. The evidence of such superiority has vanished for ever.

There are, however, three useful archaeological possibilities, which can be used, armed with plenty of imagination, to increase one's understanding of what might be called our food past. The first is the shop which used at one time to sell food – the baker, the dairyman, the butcher, the greengrocer, even the chain-grocer – but which is now used for some quite different purpose. Its survival allows us to see the size of shop which was once economically viable as a food retailing unit, but which at some point during the past 25 years or so could no longer yield the profit required. Any local directory of the 1940s will provide plenty of examples of such shops. The second kind of opportunity is the shop which has, for sound commercial reasons, deliberately been maintained in something close to its traditional form – the delicatessen, the food hall in a major department store, the pub which miraculously escaped modernisation. And the third type of archaeology is the shop that simply closed and has remained unlet and unsold just as it was, a monument to yesterday. Every English town of

Mac Fisheries, Croydon 1935. Fish and poultry retailing in the old way

any size contains examples of all three, but far and away the richest field for anyone who wants to find out for himself what food shopping was like in pre-supermarket days is the Republic of Ireland. Here, and especially in the West, one can get the authentic feel of old-style shopping to an extent which is rarely possible in England.

The great destroyer of both records and archaeology – not only, of course, in food retailing – has been the tidal wave of mergers which has been a feature of the commercial history of the post-1945 period. Both the individual shop and the chains have suffered from this process. The creation of the giant grocery concern, Allied Suppliers, is the outstanding example. Few people outside the trade have ever heard of Allied Suppliers, since it operates no shops under its own name. Of the six separate chains of food shops which went to make Allied Suppliers, only one, Liptons, has been allowed to keep its public face. The history of the six covers 150 years. The oldest, the Maypole Dairy, was established in 1819 and passed under the control of the Home and Colonial in 1924, although it continued to trade under its own name. Liptons, which began in Glasgow in 1871, was taken over by Van den Berghs, the international margarine firm, in 1927 and then, four years

*Mac Fisheries – fish retailing goes hygienic.
By the 1950s most branches had glassed-in
windows and marble-topped counters.
Fruit and vegetables were also starting to be
sold*

*Mac Market, Brentwood, Essex. Fish
ceases to be king*

later, by the empire-building Home and Colonial. The Newcastle-based Meadow Dairy Co. (1901) was bought by Van den Berghs in 1912 and was absorbed by Home and Colonial in 1929. Pearks Dairies (1860) was bought by Meadow Dairy in 1914. Home and Colonial itself started business in 1885 and was taken over in 1919 by the second great margarine group, Jurgens. In 1959 Home and Colonial, now the owner of all six once independent chains, became Allied Suppliers, and the English grocery scene was never to be the same again.

The names are one thing and the archaeology another. Many of the old Home and Colonial, Maypole, Meadow Dairy, Liptons and Pearks shops were either destroyed by wartime bombing or have since been pulled down under urban redevelopment schemes. But many of the 2000 still remain and now operate as fashion shops, electrical shops, record shops, shoe shops, wine and spirit shops or any other kind of shop which, under today's economic conditions, can carry on a satisfactory business with 500 or 1000 square feet of selling space.

One old-established and well-known food chain, the Mac Fisheries, has survived with most of its branches intact by transforming the character of its business. Its original conception in 1919 was bizarre and some fairly rapid change was inevitable. The brainchild of the first Lord Leverhulme, its original main purpose was to sell herrings caught by the men of the islands of Lewis and Harris, which were experiencing economic difficulties. With this aim in mind, Lord Leverhulme bought 300 shops and a fleet of herring drifters. The previous owners of the shops were kept on as Mac Fisheries managers and left more or less to their own devices. The scheme, not surprisingly, failed and within a few years the chain had been reorganised along more conventional lines. It is now part of the Unilever group, which maintains reasonably good records of its subsidiary companies.

What has happened to Mac Fisheries during the past 25 years reflects the revolution in the fish trade itself. In 1950, even the smallest English town had a shop where one could buy fresh fish. Since then the majority of fish shops have disappeared – once again the local directories tell the story – and it is now difficult to discover such a shop. Mac Fisheries had a great many competitors 20 years ago, but few remain now. As many of us remember and as the photographic archives testify, the Mac Fisheries shops sold almost exclusively fish and poultry until the mid-fifties. Since then, fish has been available more conveniently and appealingly as frozen fillets and as fish fingers and the traditional wet fish trade has declined considerably, both to households and to the catering market. In order to survive and to keep what fish business remained, Mac Fisheries became retailers of fruit and vegetables, taking over half of each shop for the purpose. By keeping the sales area small – very small by modern standards – the profitability of the branch could, at least in theory, be increased, but at the price of considerable congestion and of exceedingly hard work on the part of the staff. The Mac Fisheries is very rare among food chains

in that nearly everything it sells has to be weighed and served by assistants on the spot, which is a form of living archaeology. One can, however, recapture much of the old fish-and-poultry atmosphere of both Mac Fisheries and the trade in general by visiting and studying one of the select group of shops run by the Company under the up-stage name of Charles Saunders. It should be pointed out, however, that Mac Fisheries have recently been experimenting with super-markets. The days of the traditional-sized Mac Fisheries shop may quite possibly be coming to an end.

The food supermarket is essentially a place in which one can buy practically all one's food requirements at the same time and under one roof. It reproduces for the masses all over the country what the London well-to-do have been able to enjoy since the beginning of the century. Fortnum and Mason and the famous food halls at Harrods and Selfridges have always provided a range of food and drink a good deal wider than one can find at even the best of supermarkets today, but at prices which only the upper levels of society could afford. One has to make the right comparisons. It is one thing to supply a single large shop, catering for a fairly narrow social band and with easy access to Smithfield, Covent Garden (as it was then) and Billingsgate markets and something quite different to organise a distribution system for 200 or more branches scattered over a large part of Britain and meeting at least some of the needs of all social classes. Tesco and Sainsbury may not rise to the level of Fortnum and Mason, but they are much superior to nearly all the provincial and suburban foodshops of the pre-1939 period.

It is interesting to observe that neither of the firms which were most prominent in pre-war multiple trading, Woolworths and Marks and Spencer, was involved in food retailing until after the war. These two companies, Woolworths with 988 stores and Marks and Spencer with 252, now rank among Britain's leading sellers of foodstuffs. Of Marks and Spencer's total turnover of £840 million in 1976, 30% was in food.

Tesco deserves the credit for three significant innovations in food retailing in this country – Tesco House (1935), the first modern food warehouse in Britain, with centralised stock control and designed to serve 200 branches; the establishment in the early 'thirties of an own-brand system for a wide range of packaged goods; and the freezing and jam-making business set up at Tesco's fruit farms at Goldhanger, Hertfordshire. This was sold in 1957 and now belongs to the Cadbury-Schweppes group. Much expanded since its Tesco days, it is now the largest canner of own-label fruit and vegetables for British supermarkets.

Tesco never aimed at or achieved the badge of middle-class respectability, which was worn by many, if not all of Sainsburys' shops. The background of the two founding families could hardly have been more different. Jacob (Jack) Cohen, who created Tesco, was the son of an East End tailor who emigrated to Britain from Poland. After the First World War Jack Cohen set up as a street trader. 'Tesco' was

Department store food shopping for the London well-to-do. Selfridges Food Hall in the early 1920s. The Food Hall still survives and prospers, but the present style shows a radical change from what pre-war shoppers expected

Harrods Meat Hall – a rare Victorian survival, complete with prestigious tiles

Tesco's beginnings, in the 1930s

Early 1960s. Tesco moves into pre-packaging and limited self-service

registered in 1924 as a brand name by the tea-merchant, T. E. Stockwell. The trade mark was transferred to Cohen in 1931 – for some reason he paid nothing for it – and he started to operate as 'Tesco Stores – the Modern Grocers'. The business was registered as a private company in 1932, with the first store at Burnt Oak and the second at Becontree. Others soon followed at Tolworth and at Queen's Road, Watford.

The technique in those early days was to find shops at low rents in the new suburban developments around London. Estates were going up everywhere and the developers, anxious to get their shops let as quickly as possible, were often prepared to pay the cost of shop fitting. By 1938 there were 100 shops, with the methods of display changing all the time. Cohen was always on the lookout for new ideas and in search of them he paid two very fruitful visits to America, one in 1935 and the other in 1936. On the second occasion he saw self-service in action for the first time and became very excited by its possibilities. His own pilot self-service store was a tiny one at 67A St Peter's Street, St Albans. It was not a success for some time. Realising that a profitable self-service enterprise required a great deal more capital, he went public and Tesco Stores (Holdings) Ltd was set up in 1947. Self-service really took off for him in 1950 and by the end of that year Tesco had converted 20 shops.

Tesco in the world of trading stamps – a shop front of the late 1960s. In more recent years the stamps have gone, price cutting has returned and Tesco has gone back to its roots

Jack, now Sir Jack, Cohen – he was knighted in 1969 – saw perhaps more clearly than anyone else at the time that economic circumstances were making help-yourself shopping inevitable. Wages had begun rising sharply – before the war he could get good managers at £3–£4 a week, helped by girls glad to work for 25s. – and cost inflation was pushing up sales without corresponding rises in profit margins. Self-service provided the opportunity to increase the volume, rather than just the value of trade and to make very significant cuts in staff costs at the same time.

Throughout the 'fifties and 'sixties Tesco steadily bought up existing chains of food shops, built new supermarkets with car parks, a new headquarters and a warehouse at Cheshunt, equipped with advanced handling methods. By 1975 it had an annual turnover of more than £500 million. In the 'seventies it moved into the Superstore and Hypermarket age, with the Superstores averaging 35,000 square feet of sales area and the first Hypermarket at Irlam, near Manchester, with 73,000. At present it has about 750 separate centres, with separate clothes and furniture stores, freezer food centres, bakeries, packing stations and food processing factories. In the process of moving from cut-price, brash, strident High Street trading to the operation of a modern type of department store, Tesco has been changing both its aims and its image. A study of the company over what is now close to half a century is an economical way of coming to grips with what has been happening to British food retailing during this period. Most unfortunately, and to the great regret of the Company itself, the Tesco archive is far from satisfactory. Pre-war photographs of Tesco shops are exceedingly rare and so are pictures of the interiors of the early self-service stores. Since 1950, however, the record is much better and the historian of the Company is likely to find the second 25 years of its development much easier to write about than the first. With a concern so continuously geared to present and future achievements, it may seem a little strange to talk about archaeology. But since, even with Tesco, changes cannot take place all at once, there is always some archaeology, some building which is a reminder of yesterday. That yesterday may not be very far back, but, relative to Tesco's development, it is still yesterday and therefore to be studied while it still exists. One such piece of Tesco archaeology is still to be seen at the moment of writing (1977) in the form of the very small and somewhat antique food store in Battersea Park Road, but its days are undoubtedly numbered, and those with an interest in such matters should visit it while they can.

It would have been almost impossible for bread to escape the processes of standardisation and packaging which have overtaken other types of food. In some ways, this is a welcome development. Bread traditionally and inevitably received a great deal of handling, both at the bakery and in the shops, and the hygiene of this was open to question, more particularly since most bread is not cooked in any way after it reaches the customer. In the days when the bakery was behind the shop, this might not have mattered so much, but once large-scale plant-baking became normal the danger to health greatly increased. This did not become a real problem until the end of the nineteenth century, with the growth of something quite new – wholesale baking. This was pioneered in Scotland by the United Co-operative Baking Society of the Clydeside, which was set up in 1869 by a group of separate retail companies. By 1900 most of the larger retail co-operative societies in Scotland were receiving daily deliveries of bread from the central bakery in Glasgow. In England there was nothing really comparable before the present century. The Aerated Bread Company, founded in 1862, supplied bread and flour confectionery to its branch shops in London and so did J. Lyons and Co., whose first branch was opened in 1894.

Centralised, plant baking could only develop with the introduction of suitable machinery, which became available between 1880 and 1910. The main inventions were for ovens heated by steam-pipes – hence the somewhat puzzling name 'steam bakery' – and for mixing, kneading, weighing, moulding and handling the dough. Mechanically wrapped bread first became available in the early 1920s – the wrapping material was waxed paper – and wrapped and sliced bread was on sale in the 1930s. But the importance of centralised baking should not be exaggerated. As late as 1950 half the bread, buns and cakes sold in Britain were still being baked by individual master bakers. Since then, two apparently contradictory trends have been noticeable. On the one hand, the popularity of supermarkets and self-service and the increased attention to food hygiene has provided a solid basis for the growth of plant-baking and wrapped bread but, on the other, the overall decline in bread consumption and the huge increase in the price of a loaf have caused many people to think of bread as a luxury, to be bought in relatively small quantities and with proper consideration of its quality. Small bakers who have paid attention to this quite unexpected development have not only stayed in business, but prospered. Ten years ago the extinction of the small bakery, like the small brewery, was confidently predicted. It would be foolish to do so today.

Bread requires flour, and the changes in the scale and methods of baking have been paralleled by equally revolutionary happenings in the milling industry. The twentieth century has seen the almost total eclipse of the local flour mill and production of grain products is now concentrated almost entirely at a handful of major ports, Southampton, Avonmouth, Hull and Liverpool being the most important. The pioneer of the new type of milling was Joseph Rank, who, after prospering in the business at Hull, built, in 1904, a mill at the Victoria Dock in East London which had the unprecedented output of 40 sacks an hour and which could take its grain direct from 8000 ton ocean-going ships berthed alongside. Many of the inland mills continued to work until after the 1939–45 War, and their abandoned hulks – there was one near the railway at Didcot until the mid-1970s, when it was

The beginnings of bananas for the British.
Fyffes ripening cellars, Neal Street, c.
1905

demolished – are a reminder of flour-milling in its middle, pre-road transport period.

One can also see, on railside sites, the monuments of another food industry, bananas. There is one such building, now very forlorn-looking, but still labelled 'Fyffes', by the side of the former Great Western main line near to Paddington. Few people are likely to press for its conservation as an historic monument, but that is no reason for failing to appreciate its significance, as a symbol of the enormous changes which have affected the fruit and vegetable trade during the present century. These changes are of three kinds – the availability of certain types of fresh fruit and, to a lesser extent, vegetables all the year round; the introduction of a wide range of tropical and sub-tropical fruit into the mass market; and the development of a wholesaling and distribution system which made it possible to provide small provincial towns and even villages with much the same variety of fruit and vegetables which had previously been enjoyed in the major centres of population. The history of the banana industry, which is largely a creation of the twentieth century, illustrates this very well and, at the same time, throws light on the great complexity and high degree of risk involved in any attempt to modify a people's diet.

The transport of fresh, perishable produce was not a practicable proposition until the development of steamships, which made the length of a sea journey predictable, and refrigeration, which allowed the temperature of the ship's hold to be controlled. Some types of food cargo require much more accurate and reliable temperature control than others, so that, whereas frozen meat was being satisfactorily shipped across the Atlantic in 1880, sensitive and unstable consignments, of which bananas are an outstanding example, had to wait another 20 years before suitable conditions were available. Every shipment of bananas is an exercise in timing, judgement and co-ordination, in order that the fruit, cut and packed at the right stage of greenness, shall ripen steadily during its movement from the plantation to the customer. If the temperature is too low, the bananas look unattractive and have little taste; if it is too high at any point in its travels, the fruit goes rotten.

Messrs Fyffe, Hudson and Co. shipped their first consignment of bananas from Las Palmas to London in 1878. It was packed in wooden crates, with cotton wool for insulation and it travelled as deck cargo. The voyage from the Canaries to England is not a long one, the weather en route is usually temperate and the banana crop in this part of the world is seasonal, so that no winter-time transport is involved. The experimental cargo arrived in excellent condition, it ripened well in Fyffe, Hudson's cellars in Long Acre and it sold well at Covent Garden Market, which was just round the corner. As the banana imports increased, new ripening rooms were built at 9–12 Bow Street. These premises, which were certainly entitled to be called the birthplace of the banana industry in Britain, were destroyed by a bomb during the Second World War, so that the first stage in the industry's archaeology no longer survives.

Meanwhile, Elder Dempster, the shipping company, which had vast interests in West Africa and the Canaries, had also become active in the banana trade and in the late 1880s set up ripening rooms at 45 Long Acre. Until the turn of the century, all the bananas sold in Britain – and few people outside London either saw them or were sufficiently well-to-do to buy what was still a luxury product – came from the Canaries. The American market, however, was being looked after by the United Fruit Company of America, which took nearly the whole of the Jamaican crop. United Fruit had plans to grow bananas in Cuba, which would have been a disaster for the economy of Jamaica, and the British government was persuaded to try to save the situation by subsidising Elder Dempster to experiment with refrigerated ships to bring West Indies bananas to Britain. The first cargo arrived at Avonmouth in March 1902, after a 13-day crossing. Most of the fruit was in good condition, but no heated railway trucks were available and there were great difficulties in selling the bananas once they had reached London. The fruit dealers were doing very well from the expensive Canary bananas and they did not want to see this trade spoilt by the cheaper, larger and coarser Jamaican variety, which was available in much greater quantities. The problem was solved by selling the fruit direct to costermongers in London, Bristol and Liverpool at a price which was within their usual range of trade. Within a year the banana had become an item in the working class diet of these cities, a speed of democratisation that has never been matched by any other food commodity. One intractable problem persisted, however: the Jamaican banana harvest lasted all the year round and the British were unwilling to eat bananas during the winter months. This was solved by creating, in 1901, a new company, Elders and Fyffes, to look after what was evidently the highly skilled business of importing and selling bananas.

Elders and Fyffes immediately proceeded to set up its own chain of depots and ripening rooms throughout the country and to have its own fleet of specially built and equipped ships, helped by the money provided by United Fruit when they took a 45% holding in the company.

The social results of the success of Elders and Fyffes have never been adequately acknowledged. At the beginning of the present century, the British working class had, for the most part, a poor and monotonous diet, consisting mainly of bread, potatoes, herrings and margarine. Bananas were their first affordable luxury and did a great deal to lessen the undernourishment of their children. By the end of 1902, bananas could be bought throughout Britain at from a halfpenny to a penny each, according to size. Slightly over-ripe ones were available as cheaply as eight a penny.

The bombing of London, as pointed out above, destroyed part of Elder and Fyffe's archaeology (and, very sadly, most of the company's archives), but more was created during the 1960s and 1970s by a thoroughgoing reorganisation of the business, caused partly by new technological possibilities and partly by social and market changes. The group, now known as Fyffes Group Ltd, is concerned with growing, importing and selling a wide range of flowers, plants, fruit and vegetables, of which bananas form a part, although still an important part. What is of more immediate archaeological importance is that, between 1962 and 1972, 27 of the old distribution depots were closed and 10 large new ones built. Six more small warehouses went in 1975 and 1976. This change of policy was brought about partly because it was no longer profitable to maintain a large number of small depots delivering bananas to every shop in the country, however small, but also because the method of packing and shipping had been transformed. Until the late 1950s the system was still to export bananas on the stem, but the introduction of new varieties, which were more subject to damage, made it necessary to cut the hands off the stalk and pack them in cardboard boxes before they were shipped. The boxes can be handled mechanically and take up much less room in the ships and the ripening rooms. The process of rationalisation and the use of larger ships has also involved closing Fyffe's port installations at Garston and Avonmouth – where bananas had been unloaded for 66 years – and concentrating facilities at Southampton, which is now the major British banana port.

Dilapidated archaeological survivals, such as the store alongside the railway outside Paddington, serve as reminders of the old days of an industry which helped to pioneer great changes in the supply and distribution of food in Britain and whose experiments have been of great value to other branches of the food trade. It would be somewhat of an exaggeration to say that twentieth century history can be written in terms of bananas, but the range of separate industries and social developments which have been closely connected with the growth of this branch of commerce is remarkably wide. Refrigeration, the heating of railway trucks, the diet of the working classes, ship design, the prosperity of colonial territories, the education of fruit wholesalers, the growth of large industrial groups and international trade rivalries are some of them. One can learn a lot from bananas.

The 1895 edition of *Mrs Beeton's Book of Household Management* noted that: 'An important trade has sprung up within the last quarter of a century in tinned food of various kinds.' This development coincided with a boom period in exploration and Empire-building, for both of which tinned foods were invaluable, and with the sale of branded goods, the reputation of which depended on the manufacturer and packer, not, as in the case of foods cut up and weighed out and measured in the shop, with the retailer. Merely putting commodities into tins is not, however, canning. Canning is carried out in order to prevent food from going bad; putting things into tins which are not necessarily airtight is simply for convenience of storage and transport and to attract the customer. Both methods lend themselves to advertisement. In the nineteenth century, the manufacture of both cans and tin boxes was on a very small scale. The cutting and soldering of the metal was carried out by hand, a slow process, and any design or information on the outside of the tin had to be either in the form of a wrap-round or stuck-on label, or painted on and then baked to harden and fix the design. Two developments turned tin-box making from a fringe industry into a major business activity. The first was the growth in demand, especially in hot countries, where food of a European type was difficult to get and where there were increasing numbers of Europeans to be fed and with the money to pay for imported goods. The second was the rising tide of food supplies, more especially meat and meat products, from Australia and New Zealand, Argentina and the United States. The First World War brought these two trends together. Very large numbers of soldiers and sailors had to be fed under conditions where the normal methods of supply and distribution were impossible. Without canned food, this would have been extremely difficult, however monotonous a diet based on 1914–18 canned food may have been.

In Victorian times, the best customers of the tin box makers were firms supplying biscuits, tobacco, cocoa and paint. Much the biggest of the firms in the box-making business was Huntley, Boorne and

Stevens of Reading, who supplied another Reading company, Huntley and Palmer, the biscuit makers. The Huntley of Huntley, Boorne and Stevens and the Huntley of Huntley and Palmer were brothers, and both Quakers. Their factories were side by side on the same site and, by one of history's ironies, only a stone's throw from the present headquarters of the Metal Box Company. Huntley, Boorne and Stevens were the first firm in Britain to combine tin-box making with tin-printing, although the printing side of the business was relatively unimportant for many years. In 1883 they were making 10,000,000 plain tins a year, using steam-driven machinery.

A Carlisle firm of printers, Hudson Scott, began transfer printing on tinplate in 1876, with Carrs, the local biscuit firm, as a good customer from the beginning. It was highly desirable to have a box-manufacturer and a food manufacturer more or less side by side, since tin boxes, particularly those of the size of biscuit boxes are an expensive way of transporting air. When they have to be moved, it makes better economic sense to have them filled with biscuits.

The Quaker influence in tin-box making and printing was pronounced. The partners at Barclay and Fry, the London printers, who did a great deal of work for the tobacco companies, especially W. D. and H. O. Wills, and for tea merchants were both Quakers, and so were the Barringers, of Mansfield. They were the leaders of a group of firms which provided certain of the food and luxury trades with what would now be called a complete packaging service, designing, printing and making tins for their customers. They were joined in the 1880s by W. B. Williamson and Sons of Worcester, who were fortunate enough, in 1886, to invent the tin with a cutter lid for packing cigarettes and tobacco. A spike, pushed from the top of the lid, could be turned round to cut the circumference of the air-tight foil layer underneath. So long as the patent lasted, they agreed to supply the tin only to Wills and it made a fortune for both of them.

In 1922 four of the leading tin-box makers, including Hudson Scott and Barclay and Fry merged to form Allied Tin Box Makers, which later changed its name to Metal Box and Printing Industries. At that time, Britain was technically a long way behind the United States, which had been using automatic canning machinery since 1895, although it was not introduced into Britain until 1927. The rumour that two of the largest American companies were planning to set up factories in Britain caused Metal Box to defend its position by establishing itself as a can manufacturer on the American scale. A completely new factory was built at Worcester to make open-top cans, ready for filling and sealing at the cannery. When the factory came into operation in 1930, 86% of its production went to firms processing fruit and vegetables, and 8% to Heinz for baked beans.

By 1939 Metal Box had a virtual monopoly of can manufacturing in Britain. It was consequently vital to them that canned goods should have a high reputation among the public, and they were understandably worried about the poor quality of much of what was on the

Individually tested for leaks. Open-top can-making at Metal Box, Worcester, 1952

market, especially in the chain stores, to whom price was of primary importance. Once the war was over, the industry had to face a different set of problems and opportunities. On the problem side was the development of frozen foods and plastic film, on the opportunity side the remarkable growth of the petfood market. The newer methods of food preservation required paper, foil and paper-board, not cans, for packaging and it is possible that can-manufacturing may now have reached or passed its peak. Significantly, Metal Box has safeguarded its position by diversifying into the other fields of packaging.

The location of the modern can-making plants has been planned to make sure that, whatever the weather, customers receive their daily deliveries of cans. This can mean, in the case of a particularly important customer, building a can factory close to the plant where the cans are to be used. If the customer decides to go elsewhere for its cans or, as sometimes happens, to make them itself, the Metal Box factory is left in an extremely difficult position. This calamity occurred in 1965 at Carlisle, when General Milk Products, the packers of Carnation Milk, decided to end the contract with Metal Box and make their 180 million cans a year for themselves. If the Metal Box factory had been making less bulky forms of packaging, its territory could have been as large as Britain itself and it would therefore have been much less vulnerable. Can-making is also very vulnerable to increases in the cost of the raw material, tin-plate, and to any interruption in its production. To cover itself against such possibilities, the can-maker has to charge what it defines as an economic price for its product. This can amount, from the point of view of the ultimate consumer, the member of the general public who buys the canned goods, to as much as a quarter of the purchase price which, in an inflationary situation, some people may think unreasonable.

What needs to be constructed, in order to make proper sense of the history of the can and tin-box industry in Britain, is a series of maps showing the location of the manufacturers in relation to their principal customers at different periods. One would then be able to see more easily the reasons for establishing the can factories at Carlisle, Portadown, Sutton-in-Ashfield, Wisbech, Leicester, West Loughton, Rochester, Arbroath and, above all, at that centre of a spider's web, Worcester. It may be, of course, that within the next ten years some of these factories will have ceased to make cans and will have been converted to the manufacture of other forms of packaging or to some completely different industrial use. All one can say at the moment is that the highly efficient and commercially wary Metal Box Company, naturally anxious to survive and prosper, may be on the threshold of creating a second wave of tin-box archaeology, the first having occurred during the 1920s, when the individual companies became absorbed into the Metal Box merger and when, in the face of threatened competition from America, the scale and face of the industry changed rapidly. The stamina and longevity of certain towns within the industry is nevertheless remarkable. Carlisle, Worcester

and Reading in particular could fairly claim to be Metal Box, or at least metal box, towns, having been associated with the trade for nearly a century.

Other places have an equal claim to be thought of as flexible-packaging towns. Among these, Bristol is outstanding. The Robinson family established its paper-making business in Bristol in 1844. By 1914 this had become a very large concern, as a result of specialising in the manufacture of various kinds of wrapping papers and cardboard containers. A rewarding market for these existed in Bristol itself, with its important chocolate, cocoa and tobacco industries. Since then the company, now the packaging half of the Dickinson Robinson Group, has stayed close to the changing demands of the market and is established in the manufacture of every kind of paper and film-based packaging material. The Group's headquarters in Bristol, built in the mid-1960s, is one of the very few large modern buildings in the South-West to be worth a second glance. Architecturally distinguished and, in an age not famous for its finish and craftsmanship, exceptionally well built, it resembles the nearby medieval church of St Mary Redcliffe as evidence of an important Bristol business family's anxiety to present the city with a building which should be better and more elegant than was strictly necessary, which might therefore, one can reasonably assume, be a fitting and, in every sense of the word, respectable monument to commercial effort and success. The post-war age has, in Britain at least, produced sadly few industrial monuments of this kind, and it is well to celebrate those which do exist.

Bristol is also the home town of Mardon Son and Hall, for some years part of the Imperial Group, which owes its twentieth century growth to the prosperity of the cigarette industry, with which it has always been closely associated. It specialises in folding cartons and in colour printing. It still occupies most of its early buildings, including one which contains a library of all the cigarette cards printed by the company up to 1939, when the habit was killed by the war, as well as the studio where they were designed and the library where the text on the back of the cards was researched.

Another West Country town, Bridgwater, has been Britain's main centre for the production of cellulose film for more than 40 years. A moisture-proof cellulose film, essential for a high proportion of packaging, had been developed by the 1930s and in 1935 British Cellophane Limited was established as a joint Anglo-Swiss venture to manufacture this film, under the trademark 'Cellophane'. A factory was built at Bridgwater and it came into production in 1937, in a small country town with no previous experience of the chemical industry, continuous process working or, for that matter, of large-scale modern industry of any kind. The establishment of the factory brought new

Interior of Waitrose, Streatham, 1955, showing range of packaging and method of display. This branch is now closed; the site having been found inadequate for the scale of operations now required

hope to an area of high unemployment in which many people had been without work for a long time. Before British Cellophane arrived to change the situation, Bridgwater had nothing better than a few completely run-down brick and tile works to provide what industrial employment there was as an alternative to agriculture. Today, with more than 3000 people, mostly men, employed at the works, British Cellophane provides an income for a third of the town's working population which, although welcome in itself, contains perils which it would be foolish to ignore. One-industry towns are notoriously vulnerable to change and recession and it is difficult to think of this huge plant being adapted to a completely different kind of product. It should be pointed out, however, that over the past 40 years the range of materials produced here has changed considerably and that the name of the company is somewhat misleading, since now it makes plastic as well as cellulose film, as well as bonded fibre fabrics. Diversification has taken place and that is certainly an encouraging sign for the future.

The point of these comments on the history of the works is to emphasise that, in its location, the British Cellophane plant means different things to different people. To older people, who remember the unemployment of the 'thirties, it is still a gift from Heaven, the industrial miracle which pulled the town out of the doldrums. To others, the presence of an obviously modern, high-investment industry in the area is, like the nuclear power station nearby at Hinckley Point, evidence of living in the main stream of the twentieth century. Others again may think of it as the Inevitable Place, the only opportunity in the district to earn a decent salary, the employment to which one is doomed. Every factory needs to be looked at and thought about in its environmental and social context, and with the imagination required to bond all these elements together into a single whole. The factory itself changes over the years and the district changes with it and because of it. One can draw a time line through an area or through any element within it and say, 'This is its archaeology at this particular moment; next year it will be slightly different and in ten years' time very different. We can study only what we see, and we are always looking at the physical evidence of a culture, which gives us clues to life in the past as well as in the present.' We could call this new subject which is in the process of developing either Dynamic Archaeology or Environmental Archaeology. Its important aspect is that it sees archaeology as a museum and laboratory of change, not as a graveyard. A building or a piece of machinery does not have to be a corpse in order to become a fit subject for the archaeologist.

There is no field in which this is more obvious or more useful than in the complex business of getting goods to the customer and in persuading him to buy them, that is, in distribution and retailing. Selling never stops and one kind of wholesaling and shopkeeping shades off into another, as new techniques of display and packaging are developed and new sources of profit and loss appear. In the present century, the history of food retailing in particular is to a large extent

Lyon's Corner House, Coventry Street, in the 1930s, with waitresses to add a touch of luxury, and make the customers feel good. For most people in England at this date, the tea shop and the pub represented the limits of regular eating and drinking outside one's home

the history of packaging. It has been a circular process. Self-service shops could never have flourished without reliable packaging; modern packaging would have been largely pointless if there had continued to be plenty of shop assistants at low wages and if standards of hygiene had remained what they were 100 years ago. The most effective way of thinking about and understanding what has happened and why, is to stand inside a shop whose shell has remained the same for half a century, armed with a photograph of the interior of the shop as it was 50 or so years ago.

The development of retailing has to be investigated over a very wide front. Shop premises alone are only a small part of the story. The kind of packaging available, the replacement of anonymous bulk foodstuffs by branded and packaged goods, the advertising which was a corollary of branding, the wide-ranging and continuous changes in buying patterns which have been brought about by advertising – all these form a chain which needs to be studied as a whole and in all its links, if one is to begin to understand the revolution which has taken place during the present century in the movement of food from the producer to the consumer. And even when one has reached the consumer, the documentation of change is far from complete. The methods of

Gayton Hall, Harrow – one of the chain of Berni Inns. Established in 1948, Berni Inns was a pioneer of the eating revolution – the restricted menu brought eating out within the ordinary British family's budget

keeping foodstuffs fresh and eatable at home have undergone a revolution fully comparable in scale to what has occurred where the food is produced and processed. Tupperware, plastic bags, foil, refrigerators and home freezers have provided the kitchen with an industrial base of its own. Whether they have, in fact, made us any healthier is a debatable matter.

three Clothing: the new textiles

From a world point of view, the history of clothing can be seen to fall into three stages. During the pre-industrial period, it was as normal for a country to produce its own clothes and the material with which to make them, as its own food. Once industrialisation had started, a new pattern developed, whereby colonial countries exported raw materials – cotton, wool, raw silk and hides – to a small number of European countries for processing and making up into consumer goods, some of which were exported back to Africa, Australasia, India and other countries within the various imperial circles. During the third stage the process was reversed, the former colonial territories developing their own manufacturing industries, with the help of machinery and technical knowledge acquired from Europe and the United States, and exporting textiles and finished clothing back to the old industrialised nations. The movement from the first to the second stage gave rise to an enormous amount of factory building in Britain, France, Germany and other countries which were early starters in the industrial race; the transition from the second to the third made a high proportion of these buildings redundant and created much of what is now known as the archaeology of the Industrial Revolution, by which is meant mainly the manufacturing capacity created by the Victorians to service the boom which made Western Europe rich.

Put in different terms, what we are talking about is the rise and fall of the North-West European textile industry which was based on natural fibres – cotton, wool, flax and silk. The decline has been most marked in the case of cotton. During the last quarter of the nineteenth century, British output of cotton cloth stagnated, after a long period during which steady and sometimes spectacular progress, decade by decade, had been taken for granted, as part of the national way of life; in the twentieth century, the story has been one of steady decline, most marked during the 'twenties and 'thirties. In 1912–13, the last 'normal' year before the outbreak of the First World War, the total output of yarn from British mills was 2000 million lbs.; by 1937 it had sunk to 1400 million. Exports of cotton piece-goods followed the same course

– 6500 million sq. yds. in 1912, 2000 in 1937. In 1937 the cotton industry employed less than half the number of workers it had done 50 years earlier, and since then the total has halved again. The woollen industry, which never had as many people in it as cotton did, has survived rather better, although there are parts of Britain, notably the South-West, in which it has died away almost completely since the 'thirties. The British silk industry is virtually extinct, and with Japanese pure silk, 33 ins. wide, being sold here for 1s. 6d. a yard in 1934, it is not difficult to see why.

To some extent, man-made fibres have repeated the pattern set a century earlier by cotton and woollens, first an enormous build-up of manufacturing in the advanced countries, where the processes were invented and developed, followed by a disastrous degree of over-production, made steadily worse by competition from countries such as Japan, where wages during the crucial build-up period of the economy were low. In the opinion of many of those best-placed to judge, North-West Europe at least may be coming to the end of its textile age. From the workers' point of view, textile manufacturing has a bad history, characterised by low wages, a noisy, unhealthy working environment and exploitation of all kinds. So long as alternative work was difficult to get, the British went into the mills, but they escaped whenever the chance presented itself. Anyone who visits the surviving cotton mills in Lancashire today is bound to be struck by the high proportion of foreigners working there. In 1975 the manager of a large cotton mill in Bolton told the author that he had not recruited a single British school-leaver for more than twenty years. His labour force was composed, apart from men employed as engineers, very largely of Indians, Pakistanis, and women and girls from Southern Italy, a situation which would have seemed impossible in the 1930s, when unemployment provided a more than ample pool of local people willing to do the work. In every country, the textile industry has rested on a basis of relative poverty. Britain is no different in this respect from any other advanced country. In the United States, textile manufacturing has shifted away from the New England states to the South, where black people provide the kind of workers required, and in France and Germany the industry depends to a great extent on the labour of imported foreign workers – Turks, Greeks, Yugoslavs, Italians – who carry out tasks which the natives are no longer prepared to do.

Tradition, even so, is important. In every European country, during the first stages of industrialisation, the rural districts provided a large reservoir of factory workers for the towns to draw on. This was especially true of the textile industries, where country people moved to the factories, officially as unskilled workers, but often with highly relevant skills, acquired as the result of long experience in spinning, carding and weaving at home, when they were not working in the fields. These workers might, and often did, change from spinning wool or flax to spinning cotton, or from spinning to weaving, but there was a generation-by-generation accumulation of skill, which made each new technical development slightly easier to establish than the last. One has observed this very clearly in the case of synthetic fibres, where, in such places as Macclesfield and Coventry, people trained to handle cotton or silk have had no problem in adapting themselves to rayon or nylon. The continuity of textile manufacturing in these areas is an extremely valuable commercial asset, emphasised in a number of cases by the re-use of the factory buildings themselves.

In all countries, the nineteenth century textile industries evolved a new architectural form, comparable in its novelty and ruthless efficiency to the medieval cathedrals and the train-sheds of the Victorian railway stations. The mills had to meet three key requirements: they had to make full use of a necessarily central source of power, whether that power came from a waterwheel or a steam engine; they had to resist the pounding and shaking of a great deal of machinery; and they had to accommodate the large number of people needed to operate the machines crammed into the mill. The perfect answer was the 6, 7 and in some cases 8-storey mill. These vast buildings were scattered across the Eastern United States and Western Europe like industrial megaliths. Many have been demolished during the past quarter of a century, many have been adapted to other uses and not a few are abandoned and semi-derelict. They are not what modern textile manufacturing requires.

To understand the history of the textile industries – and understanding involves the heart, as well as the head – it is necessary, making a determined effort of imagination, to put machines and tools back into the archaeological hulks in which they were once used, and to set the workplaces within the social context of the local community. Without such an approach, we have nothing better than a set of disconnected bits and pieces, machinery deep-frozen in museums, rows of houses orphaned near the site of the demolished mill on which they depended and which gave them meaning, a single mill in a district where there were once half a dozen, and so on. A painting by Lowry, with the human dimension integrated into the picture, does more to record the Lancashire cotton industry as it used to be in the days of its full-flowering than anything that the economic historian, museum curator or industrial archaeologist can hope to achieve. There has, however, been only one Lowry, and for the successors to cotton, we have to put the various pieces of the historical jigsaw together as best we can.

The peculiarly twentieth century contribution to the history of textiles lies in the development of synthetic fibres, which can be summed up crudely as rayon and nylon. The first group, to which rayon belongs, are all vegetable in origin. The second group consists of the mineral, or truly synthetic fibres, like nylon and terylene, which are entirely the products of the chemists' ingenuity. These now have an archaeology of their own, which will be discussed in the present chapter, but they have also provided a stimulus to the traditional textile industries, driving them on to improve their manufacturing methods and their finishing processes and, by making possible mixed fabrics, part synthetic and part wool or cotton, producing something which combines the advantages of old and new.

These changes are well illustrated by the way in which one of the greatest names in synthetic fibre production, Courtaulds, moved progressively from silk to rayon, remaining prosperous but never losing sight of its traditions and its roots. Courtaulds also demonstrates the essentially international nature of the modern textile industries, their dependence on changes of fashion, their ability or inability to identify and exploit significant inventions and technical improvements with a minimum of delay and their need for exceptionally forceful and imaginative management.

The firm had the classic First Industrial Revolution beginnings, installed soon after the end of the Napoleonic Wars at Bocking, Essex, in a low-wage area, with much poverty and unemployment and a plentiful supply of women and children anxious to obtain work of any kind. Courtaulds were set on the road to prosperity by the custom among Victorian women of wearing mourning garments made of a special stiff black crepe, a silk fabric. This material had been imported from Italy during the eighteenth century but, since it was made on hand-looms, it was expensive and only the well-to-do could afford to buy it. During the 1830s Courtaulds succeeded in making crepe on a power-loom, and the rise in production which this made possible, combined with the de rigueur wearing of mourning by the increasingly affluent upper and middle classes, made a fortune for the firm. New factories were built to cope with the demand, at Braintree, Chelmsford and Earles Colne, and a considerable slice of the profits was ploughed back into the district as schools, reading rooms, hospitals and housing estates.

By the 1890s the crepe boom was ending, although the death of Queen Victoria in 1901 gave it a temporary boost. Courtaulds, with an unadventurous, unimaginative management, suffered badly. Both the machinery and the business methods in use were out of date, and in 1894 the business made a loss. At that point, a new general manager, Henry Greenwood Tetley, a Yorkshireman, was appointed. He reorganised and re-equipped the factories and did something to reduce the dependence on crepe, but in 1904 he told the directors that Courtaulds needed 'a new source of profit'. His solution, adopted later in the same year, was to buy a set of patents which gave the company the exclusive rights to the viscose process of making what was then known as artificial silk and which was later called rayon. They achieved this for the sum of £25,000, which was one of the best industrial bargains of the century.

The name 'rayon' was not in use until the 1920s. The material was called 'artificial silk' until the Americans thought up 'rayon' in 1924 and brought it into general use. The Silk Association of Great Britain

10/-. orders post free.

Ideal Dressing Gown for Spring wear, in Rayon. Light in weight, though quilted. Lined fine material in floral design. Black, Apple, Blush Rose, Burgundy, Dk. Almond Green, Lupin, Tea Rose, Naples Blue, Bordeaux Wine. Size W.

SALE 14/9
Full O.S. 16/9

Most useful for the traveller. Easily packed. A Dressing Gown of excellent weight Japanese Rayon, unlined. Cut with good wrapover and ample in length. Printed in attractive multi-coloured floral design. Guinea quality.

SALE 12/9

Warings White Sale rayon dressing gown advertisement, Daily Mail, *early 1934*

61

and Ireland (subsequently the Rayon and Silk Association) adopted 'rayon' in 1926 and in 1927 Courtaulds settled the issue, by announcing that they were henceforth producing 'rayon', not 'artificial silk'.

During the first half of the nineteenth century many experiments had been carried out in treating various forms of cellulose – wood, linen, paper and cotton – with a variety of acids. One of the results was the discovery that cotton and nitric acid produce an extremely explosive substance, nitro-cellulose, popularly known as gun-cotton. Another line of enquiry led to processes, patented by Sir Joseph Swan in 1883 and by Count de Chardonnet in 1884, whereby nitro-cellulose could be squeezed from a jet to produce a filament. Swan's main interest was in the filament as such, for the recently invented electric lamp, but de Chardonnet's aim was to weave these threads into a fabric. He set up a factory near Besançon in 1892 and by the end of the century artificial silk was being made under licence at a number of European factories, including that of the New Artificial Silk Spinning Company at Wolston, near Coventry, which began production in 1898.

This first process was expensive and extremely hazardous. Several of the early factories blew up. An alternative and safer method, the cuprammonium process, was developed in Germany and a factory using this went into production in 1899. The first British company to produce rayon on a commercial scale by the cuprammonium process was United Cellulo Silk Spinners, who rented premises at Great Yarmouth from Grout and Co. It was eventually supplanted, however, by the viscose process. This was developed in two stages. In 1892 C. F. Cross patented a way of treating wood pulp with caustic soda and then with carbon bisulphide to produce a sticky yellow substance, cellulose sodium xanthate, which was given the name of viscose. In 1893 Cross and his two partners formed the Viscose Syndicate, which in 1894 became the Viscose Syndicate Limited, and in 1897 the British Viscoid Company. This company set up a small works at Erith, in Kent, where solid viscose was used as a plastic and moulded into a variety of small articles, mostly ornamental. Licences were also issued to a number of firms who wished to experiment with viscose for industrial purposes, ranging from coating paper to making artificial flowers.

The second stage came six years later, when C. H. Stearn, a former colleague of Swan, took out a patent to make filaments from viscose. In collaboration with Cross, Stearn set up a pilot plant in Station Avenue, Kew – not far from the present industrial estate – to develop the process. Methods were discovered and patented for processing and spinning the fibres into yarn, and between 1899 and 1904 all the national patent rights were sold off, with Courtaulds acquiring them for Britain.

The only first-hand account of work at Kew, which must be accounted one of Britain's major industrial archaeological sites, on a level with Coalbrookdale, was provided towards the end of his very long life by Edwin J. Beer, who was, fortunately for posterity, persuaded by Dr Stanley B. Hamilton of the Newcomen Society to set down his reminiscences.[1] These were arranged in diary form and contain this kind of item:

> *September 4, 1899:* 'The potman found, like me, that caustic soda dissolved his skin. The clumsy rubber gloves of those days leaked at the seams. Soda got in, but couldn't get out. Raw red fingertips in contact with viscose, inevitable in washing jars, doing viscosities and so on, became poisoned.'

> *September 29, 1899:* 'The press, full of caustic soda and alkali cellulose and too heavy for its trannions, broke one of them and the cast iron box fell sideways on to Wilkes' foot. His agony was frightful to witness. Cut off his boot, got Dr. Wilson and carried him to Hobbs' donkey cart. To mews behind Kew Gardens Hotel, where he lives with his old father, a cobbler.'

> *September 27, 1901:* 'Topham invents a gadget for drawing off the CS_2, finds it leaks, and tells Baldwin to solder it up. Naturally there is a dangerous explosion, which might have been serious, but luckily (says Baldwin) the door was wide open and I found myself lying in Station Avenue near a hot soldering iron. Baldwin's wage was shortly afterwards raised from $4\frac{1}{2}$d. to 5d.'

Having sold its patents, the Viscose Spinning Syndicate closed the works at Kew and by 1909 the Syndicate itself had ceased to exist. Courtaulds built a new factory at Foleshill, on the outskirts of Coventry, in order to exploit the patents. The choice of area was made for two reasons: the ribbon industry had established a tradition of textile working in the district, especially with silk, and Coventry was very short of employment for women.[2] Here, as in Essex a hundred years earlier, there was a plentiful supply of the manufacturer's dream, willing, adaptable, cheap labour. It was some years, however, before production at Foleshill could be regarded as satisfactory. Edwin Beer, who went to work there as a chemist, recalled that 'the spinners waded in waste and acres of land were purchased upon which to dump it'.

There were other early problems to overcome, besides waste. Chief among them was the smell of carbon disulphide, which came both directly from the spinning sheds and indirectly from the sewers, and which brought a longer series of complaints from local residents and from other firms with factories nearby. In 1911 the local authority took Courtaulds to court on the grounds of causing a nuisance. After a series of adjournments, to allow improvements to be made, the nuisance was officially judged to be at an end in January 1914.

[1] Privately printed, and published in 1962 as *The Beginning of Rayon*.

[2] Rayon factories have always employed a high proportion of women. In 1919 Courtaulds employed a total of 3000 people, of whom 45% were women. In 1938 the figures were 18,700 and 42%.

The beginnings of commercial rayon – scene outside Courtaulds' main works, Coventry in 1908, showing the 'new' building and beyond it the works manager's house, since demolished. The food and drink advertisements are also of interest

The results of the rayon boom – aerial view of Courtaulds' Coventry factory in the 1930s. The original factory can be seen in the middle of the picture

Courtaulds had learnt this particular lesson the hard way and, having decided to have no further expansion at Coventry for the time being, took care to establish future plants where the disposal of effluent was unlikely to present the same difficulties.

Foleshill stands out in twentieth century industrial history for another reason. In 1911, questions were asked in Parliament about the employment of young people in artificial silk factories. During the debate, Arthur Henderson, a leading trade unionist and Secretary of the Labour Party, specifically attacked Courtaulds,[3] referring to high temperatures, temporary blindness and, of course, the smell and endorsing the local newspaper's description of work in the factory as 'a loathsome, injurious and degrading occupation'. Attacks of this kind died down during the following ten years, mainly because of great improvements in working conditions and processing techniques, but also because the 1914–18 War brought about more of a grin-and-bear-it industrial atmosphere which was invaluable to any new industry trying to establish itself. The First World War had a disastrous effect on British rayon production. By 1913, the British output was 6 million lbs., which was 27 per cent of the world total. Production declined between 1914 and 1918 to 3 million lbs., but by 1924 it had risen to 25 million and by 1929 to 53 million. World production of rayon rose from 457 million lb. in 1930 to 2381 million lb. in 1940 – a period in which the total world production of wool, cotton, rayon and silk increased by only 4 million lb. Rayon stole the market from wool and cotton (not, as might have been expected, from silk) as the percentage relationship of rayon to the total output increased in these few years from 3 to 13%.

The cellulose acetate process was developed just before the war. To begin with, it was used almost entirely to produce the 'dope' for waterproofing aeroplane wings, as an alternative to nitro-cellulose varnish, which was highly inflammable. No cellulose acetate dope was being made in Britain when war broke out, the only sources of supply being Germany, France and Switzerland. The problem was eventually solved by persuading the Swiss firm, Cellonite, to manufacture in Britain. The British Cellulose Company, which incorporated certain British interests, was accordingly formed in 1916 and a factory was built at Spondon, in Derbyshire. Full production was not achieved here until half way through 1917, by which time the war was approaching its end.

After the war, the demand for Spondon's acetate sank to almost nothing. The Dreyfus brothers, who controlled the factory, then decided to attempt to manufacture acetate rayon. The spinning problems had been overcome by 1921 and satisfactory dyeing methods were available in the following year. Spondon then became one of the main centres of rayon production. Its first cellulose acetate yarn was on

[3] There were two other works operating in Britain at the time, that of British Glanzstoff at Flint, and that of United Cellulo Silk Spinners at Yarmouth.

65

'CELANESE' LOCKNIT
....
Knickers to Match
Genuine 'Celanese Locknit
Knickers, slightly sub-stan-
dard, good size and shape,
trimmed lace' to match Princess
Slips. Colours: Pink, Sky, Maize,
Apple, Ivory, Lupin.
A rare bargain.
GLAVES PRICE, PAIR **1'11**½
Post 3d.
*Either of these garments can be
purchased separately.*

*Glaves, New Oxford Street, London
advertising 'Celanese' Locknit Knickers in*
Daily Mail, *early 1934*

the market in 1921, under the brand name of Celanese. British Cellulose became British Celanese in 1923. It made its own fabrics and made-up garments at Spondon and spent a great deal of money on advertising them. Courtaulds began producing acetate yarn at Little Heath, Coventry in 1927, selling it under the name Seraceta. Celanese sued them, but after long drawn out litigation the courts finally held that the Celanese patents were without substance. Throughout the 1930s, however, Celanese continued to dominate the market, with nearly 80% of total cellulose acetate sales. Most cellulose acetate yarn was made up into dress fabrics and women's underwear. Courtaulds eventually bought British Celanese, together with five other rayon firms in 1957. Acetate rapidly overhauled viscose and by 1939 it had 75% of the market.

Apart from the introduction of cellulose acetate, there were two major lines of development in rayon production during the 'twenties and 'thirties. The first was a series of improvements in viscose filament yarn and the second the manufacture on a large scale of viscose staple fibre. On the yarn side, research was concentrated on high tenacity yarn for industrial purposes, especially for tyres, and on dulled yarn for the fashion trade and for stockings. The shiny nature of the early rayon fabrics – rayon was called artificial silk with good reason – had not made them universally acceptable. Rayon was, to put the matter more plainly, considered distinctly vulgar and plebeian in some circles. Staple fibre was a very big step forward. It changed the economic basis of the industry and greatly extended the range of uses to which rayon could be put. Staple, no matter what raw material one starts with, consists of short threads. These are bundled up and sold for spinning into fibre. Rayon staple originated as an accident. The production of continual filament involved, in the earlier days, a great deal of waste in the form of a tangled mass of short threads, not unlike cotton wool. Bales of cleaned rayon waste were, in fact, being sold during the 1914–18 War as 'artificial cotton'. The innovation consisted of deliberately chopping up the filament into short lengths and selling it as staple, which could be spun into a very saleable substitute for wool and cotton. Between 1929 and 1939 Courtaulds' sales of staple fibre, of which they were the only British producers, increased from 2 million lbs. a year to 60 million lbs.

In outlining the history of the British rayon industry one should not overlook the many small firms which were involved during the interwar period, especially in the 'twenties. Between 1905 and 1939 rayon, filament or staple, of one type or another, is known to have been manufactured at 36 different centres. Sixteen of these had ceased production by the outbreak of the Second World War, and two more have gone since. The archaeology of the industry is consequently widely distributed. The sites may be set out in four groups. Those factories belonging to Courtaulds at the dates indicated are marked with a (C).

(a) *Factories closed by 1936*
Alexandria; Apperley Bridge; Branston; Bristol; Edmonton; Glasgow; Grace Hill; Great Yarmouth; Guiseley; Kendal; Kirkcudbright; Littleborough; Lowestoft; Peterborough; Runcorn; St Helen's; Stowmarket; Wigton.

(b) *Factories still working in 1939*
Aintree; Brighouse; Coventry (C); Doncaster; Flint (2)(C); Golborne (C); Holywell; Jedburgh; Lancaster; Little Heath; Nelson; Preston (C); Spondon; Tottington; Wolverhampton (C).

(c) *Factories closed since 1945*
Aintree; Flint.

(d) *Factories opened since 1945*
Carrickfergus; Grimsby.

Many of these factories were very small and undercapitalised, and can have had little real chance of success. A typical example was the Western Viscose Silk Company which set up in business at Barton Hill, Bristol in the early 'twenties, taking over part of the buildings of the Great Western Cotton Mill for the purpose. Working conditions were far from good, and the launching of 'Wescosyl, the British-made artificial silk' brought a legal action from Courtaulds, for the infringement of their patents. The court found in favour of Courtaulds, Western Viscose were ordered to 'deliver up the offending yarn' and went bankrupt.

The links between the old textiles and the new are of several kinds. The most important are the fact that rayon machinery was made by firms who already had very long experience of supplying the cotton and woollen industries and the willingness, voluntary or induced, of established textile manufacturers to try the new yarns. There is no doubt that Courtaulds' great success with rayon was due mainly to the fact that they understood textiles and the textile market. American industrialists failed in their attempts to exploit exactly the same patents because they were chemical manufacturers, not textile people. Two examples of the overlap between the old textile world and the new will illustrate the point.

In 1903, one of Britain's leading designers and manufacturers of textile machinery, Dobson and Barlow, of Bolton, fitted up a complete cuprammonium plant at Sydowsaue in Germany. It comprised three spinning machines of 50 spindles each, mixing tanks, presses, washing machines, pumps, churns and kneaders – utterly different equipment from anything which had ever been required by the cotton, linen or woollen mills. Shortly afterwards, they provided the French company, the Société Française de la Viscose, and Courtaulds with similar equipment. Having been involved in this pioneering in such a notable manner, Dobson and Barlow then almost dropped out of the rayon business for several years, the reason being not that they had lost

Advertisements that help you SELL

Here are just a few examples of Courtaulds advertising. These advertisements are designed to help YOU. They appear in the National papers and a very long list of Women's Magazines. Study them — *your customers will!*

Getting rayon fabrics accepted – Courtaulds' advertisements in the 1930s

interest, but that their works was working at full stretch, catering for the new European cotton boom. Once that was over, they returned to the new material and by the 1930s they had established themselves as the leading makers of rayon machinery in the United Kingdom, while maintaining a close connexion with the textile market as a whole.

The second example concerns the old-established Macclesfield silk firm, William Frost and Sons. In the 1930s their Park Green Mills, in the centre of the town, were the oldest silk-throwing mills still working, having survived over a period of 150 years the change-over from water power to steam and from steam to electricity. When rayon yarn first became available in Macclesfield in the early 1920s, the firm set aside a department entirely for it. The first people to handle and weave rayon into cloth here were therefore silk workers, mainly because their machinery was the most suitable for the purpose, but also because they were more likely than other weavers to have a feeling for the special qualities of the yarn. It is on record, however, that they were not particularly enthusiastic about it.

By the mid-'twenties, it was possible to find in the same mill at Macclesfield, old winders and weavers who had never worked with artificial silk and young winders and weavers, equally skilled, who had no experience of natural silk. This was, nevertheless, comparatively rare since the organisation of the factory and the flow of orders usually made it necessary to move workers from one fibre to the other.

Neither Courtaulds nor any other manufacturer of rayon yarn could compel firms to try their hand at making up the new material. All that could be done was to attempt to persuade them of the commercial possibilities. Sometimes this worked, but the trade was conservative and there were great marketing problems in the early days of rayon. British Celanese, as we have seen, found the answer in carrying out the whole operation themselves, making and selling the finished products as well as the raw material, a method which Courtaulds came to adopt later on. A more typical story, however, concerns rayon stockings.

For some time before the First World War, Courtaulds' representatives had tried various ways of interesting stocking manufacturers in rayon, including providing them with sample stockings and free yarn. Progress was slow, partly because of conservatism and partly because, in many of the factories, the knitting machines had difficulties in coping with rayon. The breakthrough came in 1912, when the well-known firm of Wardle and Davenport agreed to make rayon stockings. Once this had happened, progress was very rapid. In 1913 it was estimated that 40% of the rayon produced in Britain was being used in the hosiery industry, and ten years later an article in *The Economist* referred to 'blouses, stockings and neckties as the main rayon goods available in the shops'.

The Army and Navy Stores' catalogue of 1939 is full of clues to the position of rayon before war disrupted the free-market economy and before nylon arrived to create a completely new situation. In that year, the comparative prices of stockings, all fully fashioned, were:

Pure silk	3s. 11d.–8s. 11d.
Silk, with lisle tops and feet	4s. 11d.–6s. 11d.
Rayon	3s. 11d.
Lisle	2s. 11d.–3s. 11d.
Cotton	2s. 11d.–3s. 11d.

It was, in other words, possible to buy rayon and pure silk stockings for exactly the same price, a fact which may nowadays seem a little difficult to believe. But by that time nylon, unbeknown to most of its potential customers, had been brought to birth by Du Pont in the United States – a purely laboratory creation. It was first produced there in 1937. By April of that year experimental stockings were being

Whenever I see hands *(or legs)* in a stocking I think — 'Ah, Aristoc!'

Sometimes (but not often) women say less than they mean. One well-known feminine phrase of only two words may be interpreted as 'What beautiful stockings those are — how fine and dim-surfaced, how flattering to the leg. And how well they match the season's fashion-colours. How blissful to know that they will wear and wear *and wear*.' Or, to put it more briefly —'Ah, Aristoc!'

THE ARISTOCRAT OF SILK STOCKINGS *3/11 to 10/6*

Army & Navy Stores Limited General Price List 1939–40

successfully knitted from laboratory samples and in the first year, 1938–9, when what immediately became known as nylons were commercially available, American women bought 64 million pairs. The rest of the world had to wait until after the war for a similar privilege.

The British manufacturing rights were bought by ICI, and on January 1, 1940, British Nylon Spinners, a joint ICI–Courtauld company, was established to make nylon in this country. The original intention had been to make nylon yarn mainly for sale to the hosiery trade, but this was not possible under wartime conditions. Between 1940 and 1945, BNS was under contract to supply only the Ministry of Aircraft Production, and had to concentrate on making cords, ropes and parachute fabrics. An old weaving shed in Lockhurst Lane, Coventry, was converted into a makeshift factory, but the opening had to be postponed as a result of damage to the building during an air-raid in November 1940. A second and more serious raid, in April 1941, put the works out of action for several weeks. The decision was therefore taken to spread the risk by setting up a second production centre. The Ministry agreed to part of an existing ICI Paints Division factory at Stowmarket, Suffolk, being used for the purpose and this became operational in December 1942. Both the Coventry and the Stowmarket plants continued working until 1948. They were then closed, and all production was centred at British Nylon Spinners' new factory at Pontypool. This was built on the site of a large wartime hutted camp, which had housed workers at the Royal Ordnance Factory at Glascoed.

The pilot plant at Pontypool was ready by the end of 1946. It was used mainly to train foremen and chargehands until the main factory was completed. Full-scale spinning began in 1948. The factory had been designed to meet an annual demand of 10 million lbs. of yarn, but this was soon seen to be quite inadequate and between 1951 and 1953 a second factory was built, raising the total manufacturing capacity to 30 million lbs. a year. At that point, it was decided that any further expansion would have to take place away from Pontypool. BNS was already employing more than 3500 people there, and more could not be added without putting an unreasonable strain on the housing and labour resources of the area.

Providentially, British Bemberg Ltd, which made rayon by the outdated cuprammonium process, went into liquidation in 1953. Their factory at Doncaster was bought by BNS and nylon spinning started there in 1955. A third factory, at Hucclecote, on the outskirts of Gloucester, was set up in 1959–60 by converting the buildings formerly occupied by Bristol Siddeley (Engines) Limited. In 1962, with Gloucester in full production, BNS was making about 100 million lbs. of yarn and staple a year. By 1965 the figure had risen to 150 million lbs. One can illustrate the increase in another way, by noting that the total production of Coventry and Stowmarket combined was 3 million lbs. a year, roughly what was made each week

'The factory started up last year and it now employs *1250* people. It's been built round the very thoroughly gutted shell of an old aircraft factory and the way they've transformed that rather grim and fortress-like place is quite miraculous. For the past year they've been recruiting and training staff and getting production under way with the builders in action all round them. They had to do it like this, because the demand for nylon yarn is so heavy that every week's production counts.

'The factory operates continuously round the clock, seven days a week. This systematic permanent shift working's a new thing in the Gloucester district. From their experience at their other factories, at Pontypool and Doncaster, British Nylon Spinners have learnt a lot about the human organisation of shift working; how to help their workers to build their personal and family life on a new and very strange foundation that can take a lot of getting used to. The men here are certainly a remarkable mixture. I met a former painter, a railway signalman, a French polisher, a postman, a barber, an insurance agent, and, even more interesting, a lot of ex-miners from the Forest of Dean pits that have closed down in the last year or two.' *BBC radio news talk 24.2.61*

in 1965. The wartime production approached the miraculous. It was achieved by a total of only 325 shop-floor workers, using equipment which nowadays seems incredibly primitive and of which, alas, only photographs remain.

G. H. L. Andrew, who worked at the pioneer plants and subsequently set up and ran the new Gloucester factory, looked back in 1965 at the technical progress which had been made in 25 years. 'The early spinning units,' he remembered, 'possessed only one spinneret each. The polymer had to be dried in a machine which looked more suitable for agricultural purposes. All the spinning units had to be made airtight and then kept filled with nitrogen. Traces of

Hucclecote factory 1977, with all traces of the aircraft industry gone. The factory had by then undergone a change of ownership, British Nylon Spinners, the original owners having been replaced by ICI Fibres

the original 'nitrogen process' are to be found today[4] in the Cracker Plant building, which still stands on the south side of Pontypool Works.

'The early yarn was drawn on to a particularly nasty single-taper bobbin which had a tin top and a tin base and a barrel covered with cardboard. Another part of the industrial archaeology of BNS was the "pre-twister". This machine looked like a drawtwister without drawrolls and carried out the then essential stage of twisting the undrawn yarn before it was transferred on to the drawtwisting machine.'[5]

Mr Andrew is that very rare combination, an industrial scientist with strong historical interests – during his stay in Gloucestershire he was a leading figure in the county's Industrial Archaeology Society – and his influence has certainly helped with the creation of the excellent BNS archive and with the preservation of much historical material which might otherwise have been overlooked or lost. A simple example of objects which are normally thrown away, but which have been preserved in this case is the complete series of bobbins on which the Company sold its yarn, from the one-piece bakelite mouldings of

[4] This was in 1965. They have now disappeared.

[5] *Twenty-five years of British Nylon, 1940–1965*, BNS. Privately printed, 1965.

the early days to the aluminium alloy tubes of more recent times. Another and technically more exciting collection is of the glass bottles containing samples of the polymer which was used at various landmarks in the history of the Company.

On the occasion of its 25th anniversary, British Nylon Spinners went to considerable trouble to collect the reminiscences of people who had been with the Company from its pioneering days. This imaginative and all-too-rare exercise produced an invaluable historical record, now preserved for posterity.

Mr Les Pownall was one of the first three foremen to join BNS in April 1940. He was sent to America in July to learn the techniques of nylon production at Du Pont's Experimental Station at Wilmington, Delaware, and at the world's first nylon factory at Seaford. Later, he supervised the pilot knitting plant which produced 'the first pair of nylon stockings ever made from British nylon yarn. Fully-fashioned 45-denier!' and made the first warp-knit nylon underwear and nylon socks. 'I shall never,' he said, 'live down the experience of those first socks. Due to my ignorance of the way in which to fix a developed black dye, the wearer-trial boys spent hours over several weeks trying to scrub their feet white again.'

The first nylon factory at Coventry, he remembers, had once produced fire-engines and after that was used as a shell-filling factory during the First World War. 'I worked in that factory making rayon warps when I was 16,' he added, which made him a twentieth century textile worker twice over.

Alan Wareham joined BNS as a spinning technician, also in 1940. 'Several events during the first months at Coventry stick in my mind,' he reported. 'One concerns a consignment of packing cases containing machinery from America. On opening the cases, we found that all available space was jammed with tinned fruit, meat and other eatables.' The official records are unlikely to contain this kind of information, nor, in all probability, will they reveal what 'dispersal of polymer stocks' really meant. 'One job I was particularly associated with in those early days', Mr Wareham recalled, 'was the receipt and distribution of polymer drums received from Du Pont. As these were our only source of raw material, it was decided by the Accountants Department that our stock should be dispersed at various farmhouses in the district, so that enemy action would not destroy the entire stock.

'Once, when a supply was hurriedly needed, Bernard Moores and I took a lorry to a certain depot, loaded it up and got stuck in the mud. We had to unload the whole lot in the field and carry it drum by drum back to the barn, push the lorry out of the field and make for another depot. We arrived back at the factory just in time to prevent a shutdown.'

After reading a number of these stories – and every industry could produce them if it tried – it becomes clear that the development and perfection of a new process or piece of machinery is not quite the exercise in research and planning that the technical and economic

British Nylon Spinners advertisement, 1949

historians, left to themselves, might lead us to believe. The rayon and nylon industries have been just as dependent on resourcefulness and adaptation as the eighteenth century development of the steam engine. Things which, on paper, should work, failed to perform in the way expected of them or indeed to perform at all. At that point, human ingenuity comes to the help of the plan, and eventually, somehow, the wretched machine is shown the error of its ways. This is an essential, but frequently disregarded element in the history of technology, largely, one suspects, because no one has taken the trouble to collect the memories of practical men like Alan Wareham and Les Pownall.

Technical development cannot be separated from human experience or, in the case of nylon and rayon, from changes in fashion and retailing. Largely as a result of the introduction of nylon, sections of the textile industry have been revolutionised. Stockings are a case in point. The first British-made nylons went on sale in December 1946. At that time it took 30 minutes to make a stocking; the present time is less than 2 minutes. Fully-fashioned stockings have been replaced by seamless, deniers[6] have become much finer, and within 20 years the price fell from 17s. 11d. to 2s. 11d.

Knitted fabrics began to enter the market in large quantities in the early 'fifties, and soon became competitive with woven materials, especially in underwear and shirts. The progress of nylon in the field of knitwear was also helped by the development of bulked nylon yarns and of loop-raising techniques, which give warm, soft fabrics. Nylon has been increasingly used in carpet manufacture from the 1960s onwards. A great deal of nylon is now included in woven fabrics, in combination with wool, cotton or terylene. Terylene, incidentally, was a purely British discovery, made without fuss and at remarkably little cost by J. R. Winfield, who was employed as a research chemist by the British Calico Printers Association, at their research station at Accrington. The list of new fibres has certainly not reached its end. The 1960s saw the arrival of Tricel, Crimplene and the first British acrylic fibre, Courcelle, and there are undoubtedly others still waiting in the wings.

One can never forecast either how the organisation and financing of the textile industry is likely to change and develop. The position is continuously fluid. With Courtaulds the main problem has always been to establish the most profitable balance between chemicals and textiles at any particular time. In the 1960s, for instance, it seemed right to lean more heavily in the direction of textiles, to make sure that, whatever might happen to exports, there would be sufficient outlets for the Company's man-made fibres. The long-standing 50% holding in British Nylon Spinners was therefore sold off to ICI, and British Nylon Spinners then became ICI Fibres. With the money resulting from this and other sales, Courtaulds then bought two important groups in the British spinning industry, Fine Spinners and Doublers

[6] The denier is the weight in grams of 9000 metres of the yarn or fibre.

and the Lancashire Cotton Corporation. By 1965 the Company controlled, through its Northern Textile Division, a third of the spinning capacity in Lancashire, which it proceeded to modernise in a thorough-going fashion. At the same time, it engaged in a massive programme of expansion in all branches of the textile industry, in weaving, knitting, dyeing and finishing, as well as in the garment trade. To a very great extent, Courtaulds is now the British textile industry and, in that sense, nationalisation – which is not advocated here – would be a comparatively simple process.

Any process of rationalisation, however, inevitably brings heavy casualties from an archaeological point of view. Much of the industrial archaeologist's labour in this particular field consists, indeed, in unravelling the tangled skein of mergers, closures and changes of name which have taken place during the past half-century especially. The process is certainly not at an end yet, since the world, especially the Western world, now has a frightening surplus of textile manufacturing capacity, especially in the section devoted to the production of man-made fibres. One sign of this is that half the former BNS plant at Pontypool has now been disposed of to other industrial concerns. Expressed more dramatically, Pontypool now has a million square feet of nylon archaeology, which needs to be recognised for what it is, a very important monument of the Second Industrial Revolution.

four Clothing: manufacturing and cleaning

The human body has not, one might have thought, changed a great deal since 1900, but the ways in which it is clothed today are vastly different from what was considered normal in Victorian and Edwardian times. The clothing revolution, not surprisingly, reflects the Second Industrial Revolution as a whole. People walk about much less, either for pleasure or simply as a means of getting from one point to another and, in Britain at least, they consequently buy fewer clothes which are designed to keep out wind, cold and water. In countries with a colder climate, people are still compelled to protect themselves against the weather by wearing appropriate clothes, but in Britain it is just about possible to create a fantasy world in which it never rains and winter does not exist. This particular fantasy, which involves making the British Isles part of Africa or South America, has been part of the teenage revolution – one must look as one's hot-country idols look – and it has had profound effects on the clothing industry. The remark made to the present author by a director of Burtons in 1976 – 'Young people no longer wear clothes' – has a great deal of truth in it, although it needs a certain amount of interpretation. The motor car, air travel, central heating, Clean Air Acts and the wish to avoid tedious laundering, mending and ironing have also done a great deal in various ways to affect the style and materials of what it is wiser to call clothing, rather than clothes. One could sum up the change by saying that now, by comparison with three-quarters of a century ago, clothing is lighter in weight and brighter in colour, is washed and cleaned more often, and thrown away much more light-heartedly. For this new materials and facilities are to a large extent responsible – one is more inclined to wash things frequently if they do not require ironing afterwards and if one has a washing machine – but social and political attitudes have also had a great deal to do with it. If one has decided that the idea of buying things that last is bourgeois and that wearing a tie is sure proof of a capitalist's corrupt soul, one takes great care to avoid these things in making one's own life-style clear to the world.

Socially, the history of clothing in the twentieth century can therefore be seen in terms of a three stage revolution, rather than as one single revolution. The first stage, epitomised by Burtons, consisted of providing working class people with the kind of clothes that upper and middle class people had taken for granted. The made-to-measure suit and overcoat were brought within the means of most of the population of Britain. Stage two, still in progress, has been characterised by a move away from wool and cotton, towards man-made fibres, and stage three has largely consisted of ridiculing and largely abolishing such respect for formal dress as survived the Second World War. Both on the manufacturing and the retailing sides, the clothing industry has been shaken up from top to bottom and some of the results have been very painful.

Leeds illustrates what has happened better, perhaps, than any other city in Britain. In 1939 nearly a third of the insured population of Leeds was employed in the clothing trade, and of these nearly 90% were classified as being engaged in 'tailoring', that is, the production of trousers and suits for men and boys and coats for both sexes. The pioneer of the large-scale industry in Leeds had been John, later Sir John, Barran, who established his business in the 1850s and moved to St Paul's Street, near Park Square in 1867. He adopted the sewing machine on its first appearance in England and introduced the band-saw for the bulk cutting of cloth in 1858.[1] Barran provided conditions of work which were unbelievably good for the time, with regular employment, reasonable hours and wages, good sanitation, good lighting and even a dining room, the forerunner of the modern canteen. The company's headquarters, completed in 1877, had decorated Norman windows, Moorish minarets and pierced battlements embellished with encaustic tiles. One of the most splendid of all textile monuments, it fortunately still exists and is now converted into offices.

Within 10 years, Barrans had once again outgrown its premises and a new and more conventional factory was built in Hanover Lane, St Paul's Street then being used as a warehouse, cutting-room and showroom. This was eventually connected to another warehouse in Somers Street by means of a subway. In 1904 a new warehouse was built by the side of the Hanover Lane factory, which allowed Barrans, then employing 3000 people, to be more or less under one roof again.

Barrans was highly respectable – until 1939, all its female employees were expected to wear gloves when travelling to and from work. In its earlier years, it employed almost entirely British labour, but the situation in Leeds, as in London and Manchester, was transformed from the 1870s onwards by the arrival of large numbers of Jewish immigrants from Eastern Europe. A high proportion of them found work in the clothing industry, mostly working at home or as hired hands in small workshops for low wages and often in very bad conditions. By the end of the century, the Leeds clothing trade was divided into two sections – individuals or small firms making either

[1] More precisely, what Barran did was to adapt the band-saw, which was used for cutting wood veneers, for cutting thick layers of cloth. This allowed a large number of garments to be cut out at once, and at high speeds.

directly for the customer or for wholesalers; and large wholesale clothiers, manufacturing under factory conditions for hundreds of small shops up and down the country. Competition was acute and by the 1880s two wholesalers, Hepworths and Blackburns, had begun to have their own chains of shops, selling ready-made clothing directly to the customer. A small proportion, probably not more than 10% of this trade, was made to measure. It was referred to as the Special Order Department.

The large Victorian clothing factories had what was denied to the tailor in a small workshop, power-driven machinery. Until the 1880s sewing-machines in enterprises like Barrans were treadle-operated, but the invention of the oscillating shuttle in 1879 made it possible to drive the machines much faster, and at that point it became worthwhile to install steam and gas engines in the factories, the power being transmitted to the machines by means of shafting, pulleys and belts. Electric and petrol engines were in use for the same purpose by the end of the century, and the swing to electricity increased considerably during the years before the First World War, as the

The new giants of the clothing industry – Burtons' Stoney Rock factory, Leeds, before improvement

extension of the public electricity supply made it unnecessary for manufacturers to install and maintain their own generators.

The treadle machine continued for a long time, however, mainly on the workshop side of the trade. The 1907 Census of Production revealed that firms in the clothing trades had 93,314 power-driven machines and 64,070 treadle machines. Even in the bigger factories mechanisation was only partial, however, until well into the present century, simply because the development of suitable machines to carry out certain of the tailoring operations proved a slow and difficult affair. There had to be hand-stitching where the stitches did not go right through the material, as in the case of the felling of hems and the padding of collars and lapels. Buttonholes also had to be made by hand. Machines for carrying out all these processes were available by 1910, as also were a machine, introduced by Singer, for sewing on buttons; a portable cutter, the Eastman cutter, which was intended mainly for use by firms with cutting rooms that were not large enough to justify installing a band knife; and the Hoffman press, to speed up pressing operations.

Montague Burton entered the clothing trade at an interesting time, 1900, when a great deal of the work, even in the larger factories, was still done by hand, but when far-reaching technical changes were beginning to be introduced into the British clothing industry from the United States. Burton, however, was a retailer before he was a manufacturer. When he took the decision to specialise in made-to-measure garments he was running a shop in Sheffield, but soon moved to Leeds, where he set up a factory in Concord Street and quickly built up a huge business for what was known as wholesale bespoke clothes. This meant that the factory was the customer of a chain of shops. The shops sold the clothes and the factory made them, but the two sides of the business were run separately, without one dictating to the other. Montague Burton was an idealist,[2] who deplored the insecurity and squalor of most of the tailoring trade and who regarded the making of clothes to measure as a means of raising the prestige and self-esteem of the common man. The Hudson Road Mills, the biggest clothing factory in the world, was the result. In 1950, half a century after the business was established, Burtons employed 20,000 people directly and was clothing a fifth of the British population. A thousand men worked in the main cutting room and three thousand in the trousers room, and the canteen, opened in 1934, could accommodate 8000 people at a single sitting. Most of the workers, of both sexes, were Jewish, Montague Burton having a particular concern for the welfare of his own people.

It is worth dwelling for a moment on the amenities provided at Hudson Road in the 1930s. The kitchen adjoining the canteen was

[2] In 1925 the Company published, under the title *Ideals in Industry*, the history of the first 25 years. The much expanded Golden Jubilee edition of the same work appeared in 1950.

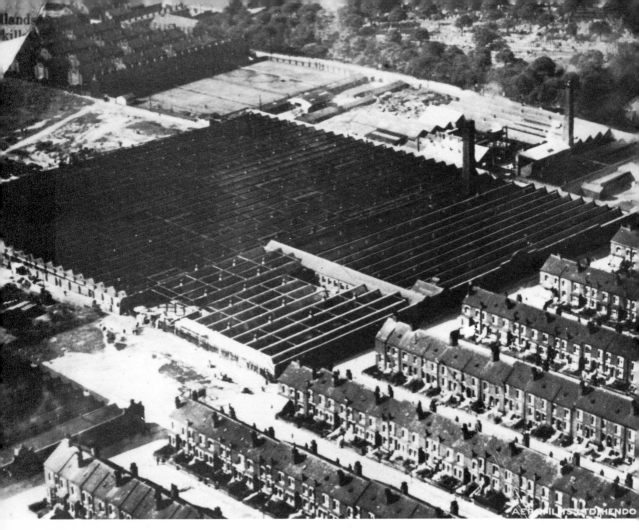

*The new Burtons – Hudson Road Mills,
Leeds from the air. The largest single
clothing factory in the world*

described by one catering journal as 'one of the best equipped in these
islands'. It had, among other up-to-date items, electric dish-washing
machines, which were a novelty in this country at the time. 'Workers
arriving by tram, bus, or train and reaching the canteen before 7.50
a.m. may obtain a cup of tea or coffee free of any charge. Each morning
there is a service of approximately 2000 sealed bottles of pasteurised
milk for milk drinkers. Hot cupboards, in which food may be warmed
free of charge, are provided for those who bring their meals with them,
and cups of hot water are supplied for any who bring their own tea.

'Each worker buys a ticket for a sixpenny, eightpenny or tenpenny
dinner, and by 10.30 a.m. the cooks know precisely what food they
must have when dinner time arrives. Learners form a special class, for
both financial and other reasons. For them dinners are served – meat,
potatoes and other vegetables – and pudding at a charge of 4d. per
meal. They may also obtain a cup of tea for $\frac{1}{2}$d. or a cup of milk for 1d.'[3]

[3] *An Historic Occasion*. Some notes on the part played by the Welfare Department of
the Montague Burton organisation. Issued on the occasion of the celebrations to mark
the opening of the new canteen at Hudson Road Mills, Leeds, October 9, 1934.

There was a Medical Clinic ('established for the treatment of minor accidents, which generally arise from needles. Finger-pricks, if neglected, might lead to blood-poisoning'), an Optical Room ('the firm has taken the lead by engaging an eye-specialist for the services of the workers, as eye strain is very severe in the case of close needle-work'), a Dental Surgery, and Rest Rooms ('an hour's rest often makes it possible to return to work, rather than be sent home'). The sports ground covered ten acres. It included a swimming bath and eight hard tennis courts.

Among the Company's social organisations were an Operatic Society, a Dramatic Society and, reflecting the Founder's own convictions and ideals, a Montague Burton branch of the League of Nations Union, with a membership of 6000 in pre-war days.

'The founder of this firm', said a booklet produced by the Welfare Association in 1934, 'conceived Hudson Road Mills as a place where labour should wear a smiling face, and any success attained springs from the fact that material development has marched shoulder to shoulder with a new generation of workers, heartened by the fresh conception of the dignity of labour.' This concern extended beyond the employees of the firm. Every large Burtons shop, from the early 1930s until the mid-1960s, had a billiards saloon above it. These Temperance Billiards Saloons were financed by Burtons and run as clubs, with their own managers, as a way of keeping young men off the streets and out of the pubs.

This vast business, incredibly to many people, began to decline during the 1960s and for the past few years it has been experiencing considerable difficulties. Management may have been at fault, but the root cause of the trouble must have been that Burtons failed to adjust itself to the teenage revolution, which involved a swing away from tailored clothes and towards jeans and sweaters, but it may also be that the traditional loyalty to Burtons faded away and that the new generation preferred to buy its clothes where they felt inclined and on impulse. The old idea, so carefully nurtured for 50 years, of choosing a cloth, being measured, and then a week or so later taking delivery of the suit, no longer appealed. What was wanted was wanted there and then. None of the sales tricks seemed to work. Shop fronts were changed, Montague Burton, the Tailor of Taste, became Burtons of London, the billiard saloons were closed down – the disposal of hundreds of full-sized billiards tables must have caused a severe glut on the market – but trade continued to decline, and the continued existence of the Hudson Road factory is problematical. Within a few years, it may have become one of the biggest pieces of industrial archaeology in the country. Meanwhile, it is worth remembering what it meant to its employees and to Leeds in the 'twenties and 'thirties. Of the devotion and gratitude of thousands of old Jewish tailoring workers there can be no doubt. Many of them live at the Home for Aged Jews, Donisthorpe Hall, on the outskirts of Leeds, to which the Burton family has been a generous benefactor.

The historical model concerning Burtons suggests a well-run, enterprising concern, thinking first and foremost of the well-being of its workers, a business run on a basis of 'the square deal' and mutual respect. Conversations with old people who used to work at Burtons, many of them for decades, suggest that the model is, in general, accurate and reliable, but that in the interests of truth and completeness it may need to be modified in certain respects. Consider, for example, Mr Sydney Silver, now in his late 70s, who worked at Burtons for 44 years and who could certainly be considered a loyal servant of the company. 'I never went to school,' he said. 'Things was very bad. I couldn't manage to go to school. I had to help my father.' So, like many other young Jews of his time, he learnt tailoring in a small workshop in Leeds, and then in 1914 he went into the Army. After the war he became a commercial traveller for a few years, 'but after that things went bad I got a job in Burtons.' This was not, he was at pains to emphasise, as a mere machine hand. He was a skilled man, a fully trained man. 'I was a tailor there. I was an all-round man there. I didn't use to go on the machines. I can do the job all round.'

He was very happy at Burtons – 'The shop was very good. It was just like going home' – but he never took any part in the firm's social activities and never ate in the canteen, 'because I was a strict vegetarian. I used to eat salads and cheese and eggs. I didn't eat no flesh.' Many Jewish people are vegetarians. It seems curious that Burtons great canteen does not appear to have made proper provision for them. But Mr Silver, it will be noted, went to Hudson Road to work and to earn his living, and for no other reason. He played no tennis or cricket, never swam, he contributed nothing to the Dramatic Society as an actor or to the Operatic Society as a singer. He was not one of the 6000 members of the Burton branch of the League of Nations Union. He was hired as a tailor and that remained his link with the firm.

Mrs Berd always hated factory work. 'I wasn't clever,' she said. 'In these days now you hear of girls going for hairdressing, telephonists and all that, but in those days, when a girl like me left school, it was straight into the factory. My mother was a widow, and she couldn't afford to let us do anything else. It was wicked. I hated it.' She worked for several tailoring firms in Leeds. One of them was Burtons, soon after the First World War. This was not, as it happened, at Hudson Road, 'not in this big place. At that time they were in Byron Street, right at the bottom, and it was filthy, filthy dirty conditions. That's why I hated it.' The model is corrected once again. Why, one asks oneself, have I never until this moment heard of Byron Street? Why have I allowed myself to be hypnotised by Hudson Road?

Mr Charles Raife was apprenticed to 'a little tailor, a bedroom tailor. That's where I learned the trade and when I were around 29–30 me and my father worked together, and then he died.' So, in 1931, he went to Burtons and worked there for 35 years, 20 of them as Head Passer. 'When the war started,' he said, 'I were exempt because I were

*A corner of the Hudson Road factory,
dressed overall for the Coronation*

the only one who understood the uniforms. I understand every type of uniform from a private right down to a general.' Hudson Road was under construction when he started working for Burtons. 'They were building. It wasn't too good at first. Bad management, not the directors, but some of the under-men. They were scheming on how to save pennies. Sir Montague didn't bother so much, he left it to his other men. The first ten years was bad, very bad. We had some very nice managers, but the under-managers tried to save halfpennies and pennies, you see.' This is hardly the kind of information one would be likely to get from the archives or the public relations department, but it rings true and helps one to adjust one's sights. This is Burtons, warts and all, and only the very naive and gullible industrial historian is likely to believe in a model which fails to show the warts.

But, despite the unpromising beginnings, Mr Raife came to like Burtons. 'I was very happy there. It were a marvellous place. No complaints about Burtons. I'm only sorry I had to retire.' His son worked there, too, but 'he wanted to be a designer, and I couldn't get him into the designer's office. I asked the directors and somehow the head designer must have been a bit nervous of his abilities, and so he put a block on it. Anyway, when he was 19, they got him a job in Belfast, where they make those linen coats, as an assistant designer. He were lonely, he wasn't brought up tough like me. I used to like going out dancing. I wouldn't have been short of company, but he was studying all the while. I couldn't believe it were my son. One of the models took him home and he were lonely and it matured, and he married her eventually.'

And that, too, helps to correct the model. Why, in a firm that was publicly so devoted to the welfare of its employees, so anxious to give encouragement at every point, so entrepreneurial in wanting the business to grow, should the head designer have been nervous of a bright young man's abilities, especially a young man whose father was so enthusiastic about Burtons as a place to work? Could it be that Burtons' arteries were already hardening as early as the late 'forties and that the conservatism which was to prove so disastrous later on was already present there in high places for those with eyes to see?

Burtons was the biggest, but by no means the only firm of its kind. The recipe of having factories to make clothes for one's own chain of retail shops was attractive, partly because it provided a guaranteed

Department store Christmas shopping in Oxford Street – Bourne & Hollingsworth, November, 1919

outlet for what the factory made and partly because the whole of the profit stayed within the same company. The four largest groups operating along these lines, in addition to Burtons, before the Second World War were the Fifty-Shilling Tailors, the retailing side of Price's Tailors; Rego; Hepworths; and Jacksons. All of these traded at the lower end of the market, although in the case of Burtons there was some overlap with some of the more obviously middle class men's outfitters, particularly Austin Reed. Of the Big Five, the Fifty-Shilling Tailors and Rego disappeared during the 'fifties, bought out by Great Universal Stores, and eliminated from the scene. Jacksons merged with Burtons, also in the 1950s. Hepworths, who adapted to changing conditions much more quickly and successfully than any of their major competitors, are still trading under their own name and prospering. A study of the street directory for 1950 of any large town will reveal the casualties which have occurred among men's clothing shops since that date. Unfortunately the archives, such as they may have been, of Rego and the Fifty-Shilling Tailors died with the firms themselves. There is some information about them, including the occasional illustration, in the files of the two trade periodicals, *The Tailor* and *The Garment Maker*, but for solid details of prices, styles and quality the only really useful source are advertisements in local newspapers.

The development of the manufacturing and retailing of women's clothing proceeded very differently from that which took place in the men's trade. Before the 1930s there was, on the women's side of the industry, no equivalent of Burtons or Barrans. If they were rich, women employed dressmakers or patronised the department stores; if they were not rich, they either made their clothes themselves or hired even poorer women to do the job for them. The development of what is professionally known as the women's outerwear industry into a complicated, highly organised system for producing ready-made clothing along factory lines dates from the 'twenties, but for dressmaking one had to wait another ten years. Before this, such factories as did exist bore a close resemblance to the workrooms which provided the couturiers with their high-priced fashions, that is, they were groups of highly skilled workers carrying out their various tasks in the same building. Then work was not broken down into separate sections and stages, as it is in a factory and the scale of each production unit was, by comparison with what Leeds had to offer, very small. Wholesalers existed, but they were relatively unimportant. Manufacturers usually dealt directly with the retailers, and, since the retailers bought on a very seasonal basis, the factories or workrooms had serious problems of irregular employment, over-production and shortage of working capital.

This system continued even after factory production became well established. A Board of Trade report issued in 1942 showed that 67% of women's tailored outerwear and 62% of dresses were at that time being sold direct from manufacturer to retailer, which were almost exactly the same as the 1939 figures. The proportion of sales of all types of outerwear achieved by the different kinds of retailers in 1939 were estimated to be:[4]

Multiple shops and chain stores	16–18%
Department stores	19–23%
Co-operative Societies	8–9%
Other retailers	50–57%

What this means, in simple terms, is that up to the outbreak of the Second World War more than half of all women's outer garments were being bought from small shops, individually owned by local proprietors. But the position was more complicated than the figures suggest. To begin with, the department stores did a large trade in piece goods, which were sold for making up either at home or by dressmakers. In addition to this, one has to reckon with the fact that the department stores, especially in London, catered for an overwhelmingly middle class public, although their 'bargain basements' provided a market for considerably cheaper clothing which was within the means of working class families. The mergers of big stores,[5] which was taking place from the beginning of the century onwards, created an extension of central buying and therefore of the size of orders. This in turn led to an increase in the size of manufacturing units.

Multiple store trading developed considerably during the 'thirties. Two kinds of group were involved, the first, like Marks and Spencer, controlling variety chain stores, and the second, like C. & A. Modes, specialising in women's clothes. Before 1939, Marks and Spencer's upper price limit of 5s. allowed them to stock only the cheaper qualities of dresses, blouses and skirts, and the same was true of the British Home Stores. Woolworths, with a top price of 1s., could achieve little more than socks and shoe-laces. Since the war, Marks and Spencer's system of contract production for all types of clothing, especially women's outerwear, has had far-reaching effects on manufacturing. Links between manufacturer and retailer are close and continuous, the very large and steady orders which are available being subject to extremely tight pricing and complete adherence to specifications. For those manufacturers who are willing to co-operate on such a basis, there is the comfort of knowing that the factory is assured of a steady flow of work and that money is available for installing the latest equipment, as a necessary step towards keeping costs down. There are, even so, certain disadvantages facing the

[4] James B. Jeffreys, *Retail Trading in Great Britain, 1850–1950*, p. 349.
[5] John Barker bought Pontings in 1907 and Harrods took over Dickins and Jones in 1914. The Debenham and United Drapery Stores groups were both established in 1927 and Selfridge Provincial Stores in 1926 – the latter group being taken over by the John Lewis Partnership in 1940. During the 'thirties, Great Northern and Southern Stores and Lewis's both relied heavily on central control over buying and merchandising.

Summer sales c. 1938. C & A Modes in the West End

customer who deals with Marks and Spencer. The first is a limited, some would say very limited, range of styles and colours. The second is the company's policy of not allowing the customer to try anything on before buying it. And the third is the sad fact that the nature of the display system in the stores – not peculiar, of course, to Marks and Spencer – means that shoplifting takes place on an enormous scale, causing losses which have to be met by those customers, the great majority, who pay for their goods honestly.

Inevitably, the great scale on which both the department store groups and the multiples now operate has its drawbacks from the customer's point of view as well as certain real advantages. A high degree of standardisation is inevitable, which displeases some people a great deal, but does not appear to bother others. The multiples in particular aim to trade right across the class spectrum, accepting what that must mean in terms of appealing to an average taste. They claim, probably rightly, that by narrowing the range of style and quality, they have been able to raise the level of what most people in Britain buy.

Those who are dissatisfied can patronise the boutiques and other kinds of small shop which are more likely to provide them with what they want.

It is reckoned by Marks and Spencer that on any given day now, 70% of British women, 80% of British children and 20% of British men will be wearing at least one garment bought at a Marks and Spencer store. Underwear undoubtedly accounts for a very high proportion of these sales. It is the ideal type of clothing to be made and sold on a mass-market basis. With something like two out of every three brassières bought each year in Britain coming to the customer via Marks and Spencer, one has approached very close to a monopoly situation.

The manufacture of brassières can fairly be reckoned a twentieth century industry. These garments were not available or thought of in Victorian times, although in the 1890s a certain amount of discreet business was being done in what were known as 'bust improvers',[6] some of which were apparently constructed of celluloid, an interesting example of the wide range of uses which was found for this new material. Until the 1930s, a high percentage of brassières seem to have been custom-built, since books contain practical advice for women contemplating making them. Materials considered suitable included muslin and sateen, and, for more glamorous occasions, glove silk, taffeta, ribbon, lace and net. 'The requisites are ease and firmness, without strain, meaning that the brassière must be cut from a proper material, carefully fitted and accurately finished for the proper effect. Care must be taken that the brassière is quite large enough, for there is nothing that makes a woman more uncomfortable than the wearing of too small a garment of this kind.'[7] This, in a publication of 1930, suggests that brassières were still regarded as a comparatively little-known innovation and anything one might reasonably call a brassière industry was still very much in its infancy. It developed, perfectly logically, out of corsetry-making, and as the production of corsetry has steadily declined, so the production of brassières has increased. Firms such as Aertex, Berlei, Charnaux, Gossard and Roussel, which by 1930 had been making corsetry for 50 years and more, found it easier to transfer their attentions, when the time came, to designing and producing brassières, a garment which, during the past 40 years, has served both as a symbol of female emancipation and, more recently, as evidence of women's subjection to the base desires of men. It is interesting to observe, in passing, that for more than a hundred years the principal centres of corsetry manufacture in Britain have been Bristol and Portsmouth. The reason most frequently advanced for this is that both cities contained a large number of sailors' wives, who needed something to do while their husbands were away at sea.

[6] On this, see C. Willett Cunningham, *English Women's Clothing in the Nineteenth Century*, Faber, 1937.
[7] *Underwear and Lingerie*, Women's Institute of Domestic Arts and Sciences. Scranton, Pennsylvania, 1930.

Of the other major changes in fashion and dress which should be mentioned as characteristic of the present century, one should instance the decline in the wearing of hats, by both sexes; the shift from leather to plastic in such items as handbags, belts and shoes; a very marked fall in the wearing of ties; and the switch from stockings to tights. All these have had a considerable effect on the manufacturing industries involved.

Shoes seem worthy of more detailed discussion. In the Depression year of 1938, every man, woman and child in Britain bought an average of 2.78 pairs of footwear a year. This included everything from bedroom slippers to football boots. In 1956, when there was full employment and an affluent working class, the figure was 2.56 pairs. Shoes in 1956 may possibly have been more expensive and of better quality than in 1938, but the market had grown only in proportion to the rise in population over the period. Women, both in 1938 and 1956, tended to have more pairs of new shoes a year than men and, at the later date, people between the ages of 15 and 39 spent twice as much each year on shoes as the rest of the population.

By the mid-'fifties, concentration on the manufacturing side had not progressed very far. There were still about 1000 firms making footwear, and the 85% of them that employed fewer than 200 employees produced about half the total British output. Only 50 establishments employed more than 400 people.

Far more concentration had taken place in retailing. The Sears group owned about 1500 shops altogether. Of these, 600 formerly belonged to Freeman, Hardy and Willis, 300 to True Form, 250 to Dolcis and 200 to Manfield. Saxone-Lilley and Skinner controlled nearly 500 shops, William Timpson more than 240, Lotus and Delta about 150 each. British Bata had rather fewer than 300 shops and Norvic, the Norwich-based concern, was firmly established in retailing, as well as in manufacturing. The largest independent manufacturer, C. and J. Clark, was developing its Peter Lord chain of shops, a process which has been continued during the 'sixties and 'seventies.

Reliable figures are difficult to obtain, but it seems likely that sales of footwear in the home market in 1957 were divided among the different types of retailer approximately as follows:

Independents	22%
Co-operatives	7%
Multiples	40%
Department, variety and drapery stores	24%
Mail order and other	7%

The main change, compared with 20 years earlier, was that the independent retailers and the co-operatives had lost ground and that a much higher proportion of the trade had gone to the multiples.

Technically, the production of shoes has changed radically during the past 50 years and particularly in the last 20. The aim of the

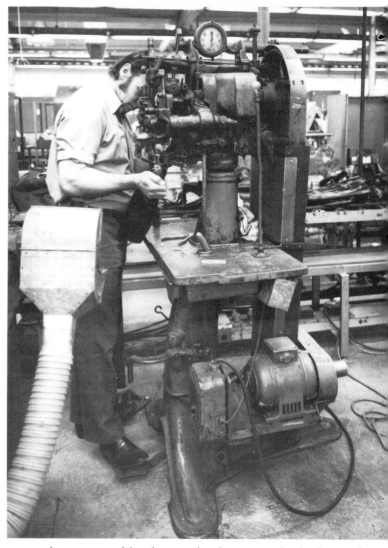

A console lasting machine, which is used in the shoemaking process of stuck lasting, where the leather upper is tacked around the insole to hold it in position whilst the sole is stuck to the bottom of the shoe. This is one of the older methods of shoemaking which is still in operation in the industry, although nowadays many more shoes are of the moulded construction

companies concerned has been a simple one, to obtain the maximum return on the capital employed. This has meant, in practical terms making more shoes per square foot of factory space and per employee Shoes had to be made faster, which was another way of saying that the labour content of each pair had to be dramatically reduced. The exten to which this has been achieved is illustrated by the case of Clark' factory, making women's fashion shoes, at Plymouth. When the factory began operating in 1957, the normal time taken for a pair o shoes was the national average, 19 days. Within a year, this had been reduced to three days. Three principles were followed. Each job wa taken to pieces and the operatives were taught to perform the smalles task which could be made self-contained. Right from the beginning every worker was encouraged to suggest how a job could be simplified or speeded up, and every suggestion was rewarded. And, thirdly, the factory was never allowed to get into the habit, traditional in shoe-making, that remedial work was a normal stage in production. Each pair of shoes had to be right all the way through the factory. It is important to point out that these innovations took place, not in towns like Northampton or Street, where shoe-making had been carried on for generations and where experiment and innovation is like to meet with more resistance, but in completely new shoe-making areas, like South Devon.

The drive for more efficient manufacturing techniques was made all the more important by the considerable increase in leather prices which took place during the 'forties and 'fifties. Effective composition materials had to be used for soling purposes, and once this was accepted the sensible plan was obviously to mould the sole directly on to the upper. This practice is now widespread, the plastic most frequently employed being polyvinylchloride, PVC. Shoes made in this way cannot be repaired, at least in the traditional sense of soling and heeling, and the only form of shoe-repairing which most people reckon to have done nowadays is putting right the damaged high heels on women's shoes. Most shoes are no longer expected to be solidly built to last a long time. 'Madam, if you want something to keep the rain out, buy yourself a pair of rubber boots', the director of one large shoe manufacturing company told a somewhat shocked lady at a

A sole being attached to a shoe by the new polyurethane rotary machine, which moulds the liquid sole onto the shoe and allows it to set, as the machine turns around on a carousel principle. Polyurethane has been used in the shoe industry as a soling material only in the last ten years, but has caused a revolution due to its properties of durability, flexibility and lightness

91

The development of the washing machine, as displayed in the Domestic Appliances Gallery, The Science Museum, London. Washing machines were not in general use before the Second World War. They became popular only with the development of cheap, efficient detergents which were not easily available until the early 1950s. Once mechanisation had entered home laundering, the days of the commercial laundry were numbered, and many closed during the 1950s and 1960s

consumer Brains Trust attended by the author in the late 'sixties, at a time when the footwear revolution was still imperfectly understood.

Shoe-repairing, on either an amateur or a professional basis, employed a lot of people up to the 1940s. Having one's shoes mended was a service required by everyone two or three times a year, while shoes were still considered an investment. The virtual disappearance of the shoe-repairer – heel-bars are not the same thing at all – and the prohibitive cost of the work if and when one can get it done are features of modern life which would have been difficult to forecast in the 'thirties.

So far as the care of clothes is concerned, two opposing trends are noticeable – the decline of laundries, coupled with the growth of machine-washing, in launderettes and at home, and the huge increase in the use of dry-cleaning facilities. Private households have now almost ceased to use laundries. The unpopularity of the work and the increasing wage-bill, coming at a time when detergents and electric washing machines and spin-dryers were allowing a steadily increasing number of households to regard washing as a comparatively easy job, caused laundry after laundry to close down during the 'fifties and 'sixties. The few which still remain are very highly mechanised and depend on industrial and institutional contracts for survival. The stages by which the washing-machine developed are well documented in the Domestic Appliance Gallery at the Science Museum in London. First one had the gas-heated boiler, with hand-operated mechanism for stirring the clothes round in the water. Then the electrically-driven agitator, with or without an electric wringer, next the machine in which both wringer and agitator were electrically powered and finally in the 1950s the spin-drying machine which got rid of the wringer altogether.

Until after the Second World War, the same firm usually undertook laundering and dyeing as well as dry-cleaning, since cleaning clothes by means of chemical solvents was not sufficiently popular to provide a living for a firm which undertook nothing else. Men's suits and overcoats in particular were seldom cleaned or washed in any way and, apart from an occasional brush or shake, went on accumulating dust and dirt from the time they were sold until the day they were thrown away. Even more remarkable and, to a modern taste, revolting is the fact that one could take a garment, a pair of trousers especially, to be pressed without having it cleaned first. The dirt was simply pressed in, so that fabric and dirt formed an homogeneous whole.

Britain's two leading dry-cleaning firms, Sketchley and Pullars of Perth, both began as industrial dyers, the first in the 1880s and the second 20 years earlier. A cleaning and dyeing service for clothes was added a few years later. Sketchley, based at Hinckley in Leicestershire,

The Spencer Mark 1 Junior (1949), the machine which revolutionised the dry-cleaning industry. This was the pioneering, totally enclosed unit, which carried out the whole cleaning and drying process in one container of modest size and which made it possible for the work to be carried out on a decentralised basis in individual shops, instead of at a central factory. The present pattern of the industry has been made possible by this type of machinery, seen here installed in a factory not, as later, locally in a shop

The present method of dry-cleaning, the direct descendant of the Mark I Junior

were not too far from most of their customers, but Pullars were at the other end of the country and their extensive dyeing and cleaning business was possible only because, until the 1940s, Britain had cheap rail freights and a magnificent railway network, which embraced practically every town of any size and a great many villages as well. As transport became more difficult and expensive, Pullars, in common with most other cleaning firms, have reorganised their business, so that most of the routine cleaning and pressing can be carried out in the local branch shops themselves. Home or launderette dry-cleaning does not at the moment seem likely to advance very much, not so much because of any insuperable problem connected with the cleaning operation itself – although the insurance companies, understanding the fire hazard, are not enthusiastic about the spread of this particular kind of domestic equipment – but because, to achieve satisfactory results in finishing some types of garment, pressing equipment heavier than would fit conveniently into the average home is required. Pressing is still a professional job.

How can archaeological evidence help us to reach a better understanding of the profound changes which have occurred within the clothing industry, interpreted as this chapter has interpreted it, during the present century? To answer this question, one has to pose two more: where, how and under what conditions were clothes made three-quarters of a century ago and where and how were they sold and serviced? It is clear that these problems cannot be resolved merely by looking at buildings but, if the fundamental questions are what;

where; how; and why, buildings are certainly relevant to the answers. A simple case will illustrate this. Suppose, as a great many people now alive remember very well, every large town had shops in which passers-by could watch a woman sitting in a window, apparently darning stockings and other garments. Suppose, too, that photographs of this are so rare and film non-existent that nobody under the age of 30 has ever seen even a picture of what must now seem a rather degrading occupation? One then asks: what were these women doing? Where exactly did they do it? How did they do it? And, above all, why did they do it? By using a variety of sources of information, including personal reminiscences and, that invaluable historical method, a letter to one or two local newspapers, one discovers that:

(a) the occupation was called 'invisible mending'. It consisted, as far as stockings were concerned, of picking up a stitch at the bottom of a ladder, and that it was carried on as a not very profitable sideline by dyers, cleaners and launderers and occasionally by department stores, all of whom believed that an action-display in the window was a cheap and useful form of publicity;

(b) the exercise was pointless unless it was carried out in a busy thoroughfare;

(c) the work was very poorly paid and very tiring on the eyes, so that only women who were desperately in need of money were prepared to do it;

(d) nobody would have considered taking advantage of the service unless it had been very cheap. There would have been no point in having a stocking invisibly repaired if it would have cost less to buy a new pair.

Mrs Eileen North worked in London as an invisible mender – not in a shop-window – between 1950 and 1955, in a team of 12 girls, 10 of whom repaired nylon stockings, and two clothes.

'The Dyers and Cleaners,' she recalls,[1] 'had several shops so the nylons were collected every day and bought in to us to repair and returned to the shops the next day for the customer to collect. The price for a repair was 1/6 for a ladder and hole and 6d. for each additional ladder which made the average price to have a stocking repaired 3/6, but people often payed 10/– to have one stocking repaired, as to buy a good pair of nylons at that time was about 25/–. We worked on a piece work basis, keeping our own books to put down every stocking repaired. We had to do £5 worth of repairs, of which we got about a third, then for every 1/– we earned after that, we got 3d. The average wage was about £6 a week.' When nylons became cheap, the job died.

[1] Letter to the author August 25, 1977.

five Shelter: materials, design and construction methods

The history of the British building industry since the eighteenth century industrial revolution got under way can be written from two fairly distinct points of view. One is mainly social, the other emphasises the technical. Here, we may say, are the problems created by a huge increase of population in a very small country, and here are the expectations aroused by a steady rise in the living standards of the upper and middle classes. And here, presumably ready to meet the challenge of housing more people more satisfactorily, is a building industry equipped with new technical knowledge, new materials and machinery and more adequate powers of organisation. How satisfactorily have the two, the needs and the techniques, been brought together during the present century? Is it possible to say that the British population as a whole is better housed now than it was when Queen Victoria died? In particular, are we any closer to housing the poor decently?

The Victorian building boom was very real. The expansion of industry and commerce demanded new factories, warehouses, railway stations, offices and shops. The expanding Empire required barracks and dockyards. Civic consciousness bred town halls, museums, concert halls and libraries. A proliferating middle class provided a never-ending market for solidly built suburban villas. The rich were happy to commission town houses and country mansions and, when they travelled, expected comfortable hotels with considerable luxury and the latest amenities. Victorian builders had ample opportunity to learn to handle new methods of construction, and by the beginning of the twentieth century the construction industry knew a great deal about steel-framing, reinforced concrete, electric and hydraulic lifts and advanced plumbing and heating. It was using concrete mixers, mechanical excavators and site railways. It knew a lot about gas, water and drains, a little about electricity and nothing about aluminium, plastics or air conditioning.

Victorian England's most conspicuous and dismal failure lay in its unwillingness, rather than inability, to provide adequate housing for the manual workers on whom its prosperity depended. It was defeated by the size of the problem and the speed with which it had arisen. The population of England and Wales went up from about six million in 1600 to about seven million in 1700, a rate of growth which was not too difficult to cater for. After that, however, it began to rise much faster. In 1801 it was nine million, in 1821 12 million and in 1837, when Britain, like the rest of the Western world, entered the worst and longest economic recession it had ever experienced, 37 million. This kind of increase could have been coped with only by a revolutionary approach to house building and slum clearance, involving State financing on a massive scale, but nineteenth century views on poverty, self-help and the virtues of free enterprise made this impossible. The need was perfectly well known. Chadwick's great report on the *Health of Towns and Populous Places* (1847) was the first of a series which left Parliament in no doubt that millions of British people were living under conditions which were utterly disgraceful and a serious threat to public health.

A number of Acts were passed between 1848 and 1890 to allow local authorities to provide housing for the working classes, but the problem was never solved, for three reasons. The first, already mentioned, was philosophical. The heart of the Victorian ruling élite was not in the job. The second was that, by using traditional methods and materials, it was not possible to build good houses at a price most working class families could afford, despite the low rates of pay in the building industry. The third reason was that the conditions under which local authorities could obtain loans from the central government discouraged experiment and enterprise. The theory was that the loan must match the asset. If, therefore, a loan was granted to a local authority for a 60-year period, it had to be demonstrated that the houses covered by the loan could be maintained in a good and habitable condition for at least that length of time. Those who were pressing for the abolition and prevention of slums consequently found themselves faced with an absurd situation; traditional-type housing was too expensive and housing of a light or experimental type was not permitted. This restriction has continued to plague both local authorities and private buyers ever since.

Tight control of building standards in Britain was brought in with the best of intentions and, in theory, it has a great deal to commend it. Nobody wants houses or flats which collapse or which are likely to catch fire easily. Before the Great Fire of London in 1666 building in Britain was free-for-all. After the Fire, Parliament passed an 'Act for the rebuilding of the City of London', with precise standards for thickness of walls, heights of ceilings, foundations, timber sizes and other details. The series of London Building Acts of the eighteenth and nineteenth centuries, with constant modifications to cover new materials and techniques, were the model not only for other English cities but for many other countries as well. The Acts and the local bye-laws based on them have always been very conservative and ultra-cautious. They undoubtedly prevent most dangerously shoddy building from taking place, but they also make genuine progress much

The end of an era – Coombe Lodge, Blagdon, Somerset. A millionaire's stone-built mansion of the 1930s, demanding a large staff of servants and impossible to run as a private house under modern conditions. It has been in use for many years as a staff college for further education

slower than it need be, especially in pre-fabrication. A classic example of the absurdities which can be produced by our slow-moving building regulations was the Ritz Hotel (1904), the first completely steel-framed building in London. The load of the structure is entirely supported on steel columns, but the sorely-tried architect was compelled by the bye-laws to make the external walls of the hotel of full load-bearing thickness and strength, even though they carried no load whatever.

The archaeology of housing, as of any other form of building, takes two forms – the houses and blocks of flats themselves, and the factories, kilns, quarries and machines which produce the materials with which the houses were constructed and equipped. Every house is a museum of building materials and it is remarkable to discover how few people have anything but the most superficial ideas about the construction and materials of their own house. For convenience, the subject of housing is divided here into two sections, each with a chapter to itself. The first deals with the structure and the second with its equipment. This separation is, however, artificial and unreal. A house is a complete living unit. Where does its structure end and its equipment begin? It is arbitrary and unreal, too, to think of a house or a block of flats as existing in a vacuum. The history and archaeology of housing cannot ignore the environment, the physical and social context in which the individual dwelling units are placed.

If one begins with the materials, the most remarkable feature of the twentieth century has probably been the movement away from the use of wood. Timber, one of the cheapest of all building materials at the beginning of the century, has become a prohibitively expensive luxury 75 years later. World supply has simply failed to keep pace with world demand, and it would be a fair generalisation to say that nowadays builders use timber only when they can see no reasonable alternative. The lavish use of timber in the roofs, floors, fences and joinery of pre-1939 houses is an archaeological curiosity in its own right. As a rough calculation, one can say that a modest three-bedroomed house or flat would now, in 1977, cost at least 20% more if it included timber on the pre-1939 scale. Metal window frames, solid floors, hardboard instead of plywood doors, much lighter roof-trusses, wire fencing or no fencing at all – the flight from wood is something the builder of the 'twenties and 'thirties could never have forecast or imagined.

There are a number of interesting historical changes to observe in the importing, storage and processing of timber. Fifty years ago the typical system was something like this. A consignment of sawn timber would arrive at a British port from North America or the Baltic and be unloaded into railway trucks or occasionally into barges. These in due course moved off to the timber-merchant's premises, which were invariably situated on a rail-siding. Here the timber was stored under cover and transported by lorry, horse-drawn vehicle or rail-truck to its ultimate purchaser. Most timber yards had a very local market and there were consequently a great many of them. Since 1945 a high proportion of them has closed, partly because of the drop in demand for timber, but even more because it was found more profitable to concentrate business at a few large, strategically placed depots and, in some cases, to deliver consignments direct to an important customer from the docks, the merchant merely acting as an agent. Rail delivery from ship to timber yard is now rare, and the old-established timber yards remain on their rail-side sites only because they can see no point in going anywhere else. Their present location, however, belongs to the railway and canal age, not to the motor age.

Many timber yards are combined with sawmills, processing mostly home-grown timber. Here, too, a very marked amount of concentration has taken place. The modern sawmill will bring the logs it needs from a considerable distance – 100 miles is not at all uncommon – and finds this a better commercial proposition than keeping logs and processed timber on a district basis. Before the days of motor transport this would have been very difficult, if not impossible. The results of this trend, which has intensified since 1945, have been on the one hand the widespread closing of local sawmills and on the other a significant increase in the size of the mills which survive. It should not be forgotten that a well-managed sawmill is interested in disposing of its waste-products as profitably as possible. Intensive poultry and pig production units are good customers for shavings and sawdust, to use as litter, and, with the price of other fuels so high, cut-offs can be sold as logs for the domestic hearth. In this sense, one could say that modern energy problems and modern agricultural methods subsidise sawmilling, an interesting example of the truth that industrial change always operates over a wide front.

Bricks are, in relation to the total amount of construction work in progress, less used than they once were, although every attempt has been made to prevent them from pricing themselves out of the market, but they too are showing distinct signs of becoming a luxury product. The reason for this concerns not so much the manufacturing process, but the cost of laying them. A brick is, by modern standards, uneconomically small as a pre-fabricated unit, and in the 1970s a British bricklayer lays far fewer in a day than he once did. He works much shorter hours, is less amenable to discipline, has no fear of dismissal and, with a strong union to support him, adjusts his working pace to suit his convenience. On the other hand, house-buyers are always supposed to prefer a brick house, as a mark of quality and respectability, and to be prepared to make other economies – size of house, size of garden – in order to be the proud owners of bricks and mortar. How true this really is and how much a proof of the innate and profitable conservatism of builders and estate agents it is difficult to say, but it is very much a factor to be reckoned with.

The manufacture of what are known in the industry as common bricks, that is, bricks used for everyday purposes and not intended to look either elegant or expensive, has undergone a revolution during the present century. The nineteenth century needed a great many bricks: the lining of a railway tunnel required about 14 million bricks a mile, and 20 suburban villas about the same, and a hand-moulder who made 500 bricks a day was a very good man. Some speeding up resulted from wire-cutting, introduced in 1841, and from extrusion moulding, first developed in 1875, but throughout the Victorian period the typical brickworks employed 50 men and boys at most. Since clays suitable for brickmaking are found in many parts of the British Isles and since bricks are heavy, expensive and somewhat vulnerable to transport, Britain in 1900 was dotted with local brickworks, most of which are now little more than a memory. The main agent of this mass shut-down has been the successful manufacture of a type of brick known as Flettons.

This began at the end of last century at Fletton, near Peterborough. It was discovered that the Lower Oxford Clay, which is plentiful and easily accessible in this region, could be pressed into a brick which, because of its relatively low water content – 18% to 20% – could be fired straight away, without needing the period of previous drying which was standard practice in the industry. Equally important was the fact that this shale-like clay contains as much as 10% of carbonaceous material, which burnt during firing in the kiln and reduced the amount of coal needed by about a third. Less fortunately placed brickworks in other parts of the country found it impossible to compete with the advantages enjoyed by the Fletton area, which in turn encouraged Fletton to embark on large-scale, highly mechanised production. Other neighbouring brick-making firms adopted the same methods. They included the Forder works at Pulinge, which began making Flettons in 1897. The Forder Company was eventually absorbed into a much larger concern, which, in 1936, took the name of the London Brick Company and is now the largest brickmaking company in the world. Two other companies, Marston Valley Brick and Redland (Flettons) were also formed as a result of amalgamations, and these three now produce, at their various works, not all of them in the Fletton area, more than half the bricks and tiles used in Britain.

The Fletton area produced most of the bricks used to create the vast expansion of the London suburbs during the first 40 years of this century. Croydon, Wembley and Barnet are part of the archaeology of the Fletton brickworks. Transport costs were high, but the degree of mechanisation and the low fuel bills allowed bricks made in the Fletton region – Peterborough, Bedfordshire and North Buckinghamshire – to be sold at a competitive price over most of Britain.

The brickmaking landscape, flat, mainly treeless and dominated by dozens of very tall kiln chimneys, is like nowhere else in the country. Bedfordshire alone has more than a hundred of these chimneys, ranging in height from 100 to 300 feet. Very tall chimneys – which are themselves built of the local product and its most conspicuous monuments and advertisements – have been found to be the only effective way of dealing with what had been a very serious pollution problem. Previously the sulphur oxides and fluorine compounds in the waste gases from the kilns had destroyed vegetation and produced sickness, sometimes fatal, among farm livestock. The industry's other form of environmental destruction, the creation of thousands of acres of vast pits from which the clay had been extracted, is being dealt with partly by filling in the pits with London's refuse – each acre of clay pit takes 50,000 tons of rubbish – and partly by tidying up and landscaping the pits, so that they can be used for water sports.

Some of the Fletton brickworks have been closed and are themselves now technological monuments. The largest single complex, however, at Stewartby, Bedfordshire, is still operational, although changes in production techniques have brought about a considerable decrease in the number of men required. Stewartby was called Pulinge until the 1920s. The modern village which adjoins the works was named after two chairmen, Sir P. Malcolm Stewart and Sir Hailey Stewart, of what later became the London Brick Company. The first houses here, in the brick industry's first and only garden village, were built in 1926 and there are now about a thousand inhabitants, many of them pensioners.

The sand and gravel pits surrounding London and stretching out as far as Reading along the Thames valley to the west are evidence of the insatiable hunger of the metropolis for concrete aggregate. A number of these pits, too, have been given a park-like setting in recent years and are now used for sailing. What is less well-known is that much of the concrete used during the 1920s and 1930s in the construction of London's new housing estates, expecially in the north-western suburbs, contained an aggregate made by the simple expedient of burning the clay which had been excavated from the foundations of the houses and from the roadways and sewers. The clay was thrown up into great heaps, with coal dust sprinkled liberally over each layer, over a fire that had been first got going on the flat ground. These clay mountains, known as ballast heaps, took weeks to burn themselves out and cool down, and while they were still active the characteristic smell was noticeable over a wide area. This kind of aggregate, used mainly for the under-floor screed, would no longer be tolerated by the local authorities, but it was a way of keeping costs down and, as an indigenous material, it had something to commend it. No picture of such a heap is known to exist – all construction photographs of pre-war suburban housing are very rare – and, so far as one can discover, there is no printed record. This is an interesting case of memory and oral history providing the only form of documentation of a technique widely used no more than 40 years ago.

By today's standards, most of the suburban houses of the 'twenties and 'thirties were not particularly comfortable places to live in. The rooms were small, the heating arrangements were not distinguished, and the workmanship and materials frequently left a great deal to be desired. As examples of building craftsmanship they did not compare with the new houses in the inner suburbs of the major cities which the middle classes were buying and renting before the First World War. Some of the interwar suburban houses were, of course, very well built, but most of them were designed, usually without the benefit of an architect, to yield the maximum possible profit to the builder and at the same time to sell quickly in a highly competitive market. The faults did not take long to show up and during the years since 1945 in particular – not much was possible during the war – a high proportion of these jerry-built houses have been repaired, improved and modernised to an extent which would make them almost unrecognisable to the gamblers who built them in the first place. Many others, alas, have gone downhill steadily and have become the crumbling slums they were always destined to be. In design, materials, craftsmanship and equipment, the speculative estates of the late 'twenties and the 'thirties represent English house-building in one of its worst periods. It is easy to say, 'What else could you expect for £800 or £1000?' but this is largely irrelevant. What happened, in effect, was that the Garden City concept, publicised and realised by idealists at Letchworth, Bournville and Welwyn, was debased and destroyed by men whose sole aim and interest was profit. The people who bought their houses were sold a caricature of a Garden City and led to believe

The great suburban explosion – semi-detached houses at Welwyn Garden City, built c. 1925

that it was the genuine article. The results are there for the archaeologist to study, a task which has so far been strangely neglected. There are many significant details to be observed – the garages built across the former, much advertised side entrance; the cheap standardised front doors that have long since had to be replaced; the new tiles to keep the roof weathertight; the metal window frames to take the place of the original wooden ones which rotted; the bits and pieces of coloured and leaded window to add a touch of class to the composition. One pre-1939 feature which has in most cases perforce remained is the pebble-dash rendering on the upper storey and sometimes, in very cheap houses, on the bottom storey as well. This technique, developed to cover up poor quality bricks, is almost never seen nowadays. It consisted of first giving the brickwork a rough cement and sand rendering which was allowed to dry, and then adding a second rendering which had pebbles thrown generously at it while it was still wet. Pebble-dash was quick, cheap, covered a multitude of sins and, like the gable-ends and mock half-timbering, was reckoned to give a little exotic variety to the appearance of the house.

One important detail of houses built before 1939 is only to be observed when the building, or part of it, is demolished. In most cases, the bricks or stones were laid in a lime-sand mortar, not in a mortar containing cement. This was traditional, much cheaper and, under

103

Buying one's own house in 1929

most conditions, gave perfectly satisfactory results, provided that the joints were kept well pointed with a cement mix. Once the pointing began to crack and fall out, however, it was easy for rain to get into the wall and wash out the mortar. This not infrequently occurred and has been the source of a great deal of trouble with pre-war houses. Nowadays, the art of making lime mortar has been almost lost, at least in Britain. The use of a Portland cement-sand mix is universal.

It is curious that British builders and architects have been reluctant to make much use of hollow clay bricks and blocks in house construction, although such blocks have been available for more than a century and are extensively used on the Continent, especially for partition walls. The concrete block, however, has been much more highly regarded. Within the past 30 years, concrete blocks have become one of the most popular of all building materials in this country. They have completely replaced lath and plaster and brickwork for internal party-walls. Before the Second World War, there was no concrete block-making industry, in the modern sense of the term. When blocks were used, they were generally made on the site. Hand-operated block-making machines were on the market well before the end of the century, although they produced, for the most part, large slabs nine inches thick and up to 32 inches long, more than twice the size of what we are nowadays accustomed to think of as concrete blocks. During the 1939–45 war, when all building materials were in short supply, modern-sized blocks were much used by the Government for simple, single-storey buildings. They were quick to lay, but expensive, although under wartime conditions cost was not of prime importance. Since that time, rising labour costs and the establishment of large plants to make blocks have made blocks cheaper to use than bricks, despite great increases in the price of cement.

On the whole, mass concrete has been much less used in Britain for housing purposes than on the Continent, although the need to reduce costs, especially for working class houses, has stimulated a number of experiments. In the 1920s, there was some interest in no-fines, or cellular concrete, which contained a very small proportion of cement. Such concrete was necessarily exceptionally coarse and it had to be plastered on both sides, but it was cheap and had good insulating properties. Fifty two-storey houses were built in this way in Edinburgh in 1923 and there were other instances during the later 'twenties and in the 'thirties. The method has been very little used for housing since 1939.

A different kind of concrete building block, known rather grandly and misleadingly as reconstituted or reconstructed stone, has become extremely popular during the past 25 years or so, although it was known and used long before the Second World War. It consists usually of an ordinary block of rough concrete, faced with smooth concrete which has a particular crushed stone – Bath, Portland, Ham Hill, and so on – as its aggregate. If required, the complete block can be made with the stone aggregate. By choosing the aggregate stone carefully, it is possible to simulate the natural stone of the area and in this way to achieve what appears to be a stone-built house at a much lower cost. Experience has shown, however, that although reconstructed stone, if properly made, can be very hard-wearing – better, in some instances, than natural stone – it stains, but does not weather. This gives a reconstructed stone wall a hard, band-box look, even after many years. It never achieves the mellowness of natural stone, which many people would regard as a drawback, both for buildings and for garden ornaments, for which it is much used. For interior work, such as fireplaces, the disadvantage is much less serious. One does not normally expect or want the inside of one's house to weather.

Without reconstructed stone, on the other hand, a great deal of the repair work which has been carried out on old buildings in recent years would not have been possible. The present cost of carving ornamental stone vases, finials and pilasters in natural stone is higher than many owners can afford, and it is considerably cheaper to make a mould and to cast the new work in the type of concrete just described.

Reconstructed stone, whether in the form of faced blocks or of solid, front to back concrete, has become big business, since 1945. Some firms achieve a much higher standard of finish and durability than others and a high proportion of the work carried out during the past 30 years, to say nothing of what happened during the 'twenties and 'thirties, was distressingly bad and does not bear close inspection today. This is a twentieth century industry which has had to learn by its mistakes, and there have been both fortunes and bankruptcies on the way. One example, studied in some detail, will illustrate how a new product develops, in a context of conservatism, building regulations and commercial pressures. Others, equally informative, can no doubt be discovered all over Britain.

Minsterstone, of Ilminster, Somerset, is now one of the largest manufacturers of artificial ('reconstituted', 'reconstructed') stone building blocks and fireplaces in Britain. The firm was started in 1914 by W. A. H. Hutchings, who already had building and undertaking interests in this small Somerset town. To begin with, the business was called the Wharf Lane Concrete Works – the 'wharf' was on the canal which skirted Ilminster and is long closed – and it made its reputation by the unusually high quality finish of its products, at a time when the art of making high quality concrete was not well understood. As often happens, the proprietor and his son were excellent craftsmen but not very good businessmen, and by the mid-1960s the company was virtually bankrupt. A consultant was called in to report on the problems and on ways of improving the situation. He stayed on to become the Managing Director, and the remarkable growth of the firm during the past 15 years is almost entirely due to his efforts.

The new Managing Director decided to systematise a somewhat chaotic state of affairs. He divided the company into four departments: the Fireplace Department, Garden Ornament Department, Stonework Department and the General Concrete Department. Productivity was very low – before the work was reorganised, it took two men a day to make a fireplace, whereas now the time is down to 2–3 hours – and, in addition to the reorganisation, it was decided to put in a measured work and bonus scheme. Most of the men took to it, but one or two left, convinced that they were too old or set in their ways to change. 'They weren't commercially minded', recalled the Managing Director, and the phrase tells one a great deal about the problems of coaxing the old rural, craftsman-based, easy-paced, contented-with-little society into the modern industrial world.

The reminiscences of men who have known the company for half a century and more therefore fall into two parts. On the one hand there are their memories of the high quality of workmanship insisted on and obtained by the founder of the firm and maintained during the 'twenties and 'thirties, and on the other there are the personally-experienced contrasts between the old world of easy pace and small scale production and the new world of work study, big contracts and concrete components weighing 12 tons and more.

Mr White came to Wharf Lane straight from school in 1914. He had, he says, 'no real alternative'. Work was hard to find and a sensible lad took whatever turned up. His first job was to carry and stack breeze blocks and since then he has 'done everything'. Once fireplace making began, he went to that section of the factory and has stayed with it ever since. At that time, the men worked in open-fronted sheds, with no form of heating, and in frosty weather they often had to be laid off for several days. He remembers the greasing of the moulds, 'with a special grease that the firm got, a grease that doesn't mark the stone' and the two concrete mixers, 'one for your facing and one for your backing'. The foreman 'came from the lace factory when it was pulled down'. He knew nothing about concrete when he was taken on, but he had a local reputation for handling men and for getting the best out of them, and he made an easy transition from lace to concrete.

Both Mr Hutchings and his foreman had an eagle eye for work that was not up to standard. The concrete had to be packed into the mould with hand-rammers – there were no compressed air rammers, as there are today – and if something went wrong the cause was usually careless ramming. 'If you got so far up the mould and you went to go to the toilet, you came back and forgot where you left off, so you carried on ramming and next morning when you take that stone out you've got a beautiful stone but right the way round it you've got a patch that's been missed, and instead of a nice fine tight piece of stone, you've got a big rib all the way round where it hasn't been touched, and that was half our trouble.'

So Mr Hutchings cut his losses and preserved his reputation. He had the faulty stone smashed up, and told the man to do better next time. Sackings were very rare.

Mr Mead came to Wharf Lane in 1920 as an apprentice carpenter. When he was 19, he was put in charge of a gang making moulds. After his apprenticeship, he went on to make the more complicated moulds for fireplaces and garden ornaments, some of which, for special orders, were used only once. He travelled about the country a good deal, measuring up jobs to be done, and putting work on the site. In 1924, when he was still an apprentice, he went to the Wembley Exhibition, 'to erect a stone office for the Cement Marketing Company', and of course 'that was a great occasion for me, the first time I'd ever been to London'. And then there were the agricultural shows. 'We used to go to all the Royal Shows for Cement Marketing, and then we used to put up a shed, like a cowstall, put in cowstall partitions, make louvres for the roof, put the roof on.' These were the days, one should remember, when cement was sold in jute sacks which offered little protection against damp and when disasters could occur as a result of careless transport and storage. They were also the days of intense competition in the cement business, when the Cement Marketing Board was trying to introduce a more orderly system.

The picture of the development of the firm and of the reconstituted stone industry which emerges from conversations with men like this is not the one usually produced by either the economic or social historian. These are men who were proud of being able to work to the highest standards, so that the finished product was in some way better than it would have been if it had been made of natural stone, men who were indignant at the poor workmanship tolerated by rival companies, which they feel has given reconstituted stone a bad name in some quarters. They have always considered themselves to be craftsmen, in the fullest and best sense of the word, in no way inferior to the masons whose material is quarried Bath or Portland stone.

They are also loyal men, who stick to the job. They admit their worries when they knew the firm was doing badly and when closure was a strong possibility, and they are frank about their misgivings when new methods of work were introduced. 'I said right from the beginning,' Mr Mead recalled, 'that the bonus scheme wouldn't work. I couldn't see it working. I thought that, if a chap was given three hours for a job and he had to do it in three hours, it was giving him a sentence, almost. Mr Brockett (the Managing Director) said to me once, and I always remember it, he said, "Remember the bonus isn't the end of everything. It doesn't make things easier, in fact it makes things harder, because you have to see you get the same quality, that you have to control the job."'

When one is studying industrial change, it is always interesting to wonder if people work harder or less hard today than they did 50 or 100 years ago. How does one measure such a thing? How can we judge if a weaver today works harder than a weaver in 1877? One way of trying to find out, is to ask people who have done the same job for a very long time, with different equipment and under different social and economic conditions. Mr Mead, with a lifetime of experience with first Wharf Lane and then Minsterstone behind him, has no doubt that with modern equipment and better organisation men certainly work faster and produce more. But, he says, 'I think the man himself has paced the job differently, and most of them now do one job, whereas before you were a utility man and the more jobs you could do the more valuable you were to the firm.' This amounts to saying, he feels, that it is very hard to decide whether someone finishes the day more or less tired than he would have been in the 1920s. On the one hand, the rhythm of work is different, and on the other one no longer has what is for some people the refreshment which comes from switching from one task to another.

As we have noted earlier, most of the archaeology which relates to building materials and which helps to tell us more about them is to be found not at the works but in the buildings for which the materials were destined. In the case of Wharf Lane this ranges from abandoned air-raid shelters to Mr Hutchings' own house in Love Lane, Ilminster, built in 1929 of reconstituted Wharf Lane stone, and still in first-class condition, and from the Countess Wear Bridge at Exeter to the new headquarters of the Metal Box Company by the side of the railway line at Reading, where the great cladding panels, made with an aggregate of ground calcined flint, contain some of the highest quality concrete ever made.

It is clear that housing has benefited to some extent from the experience of concrete technology gained from civil engineering projects and from the construction of industrial and commercial premises. It is clear, too, that the advantages of concrete are so great, especially in an age of high labour costs, that customers, architects and engineers are prepared to put up with the undeniable shortcomings of concrete, provided the finished job is considered to be at least tolerable. Those shortcomings are easily spelt out and equally easily noticed by anyone who keeps his eyes open. The surface of exposed concrete quickly becomes stained and grimy, especially in an urban atmosphere, and the corrosion of the steel reinforcement causes concrete to crack, split and disintegrate when there is insufficient concrete covering the metal or when stresses on the concrete mass cause cracks which allow water to penetrate to the metal.

In 1938 an important book, *The Principles of Modern Building*,[1] was issued by what was then H.M. Office of Works. The section on monolithic concrete included this perceptive comment: 'Unfortunately, there is as yet no satisfactory treatment in this humid and largely polluted climate which will allow it completely and satisfactorily to speak for itself as does stone and brick.' Concrete must, in other words, be covered up, the British climate being what it is. It is a good structural material, but it cannot be allowed to present its own exposed face to the world. It needs a veil of bricks, stone, glass or some other material to make it presentable on the outside and very good insulation, together with adequate heating and ventilation inside, if condensation is not to be a serious problem. For these reasons, mass concrete, poured on the site, has never been a popular material for housing, although much better results have been obtained from using the material in block or slab form.

One of the most satisfactory experiments of this kind was the Cornish Unit house, built in prefabricated sections made of a concrete of cement and of the very high quality sand which occurs as a waste material in the china clay pits of Cornwall and Devon. The pioneering Cornish Unit house was a bungalow erected at Bugle in 1945. It was followed by a pair of two-storeyed houses at Menage Villas, St Austell. The St Austell houses were inspected by Aneurin Bevan, when he was

[1] R. Fitzmaurice, *The Principles of Modern Building*, Vol. 1, HMSO, 1938.

Pre-fabricating permanent houses – the pioneer Cornish Unit bungalow at Bugle

Accommodation in two types of Cornish Unit house

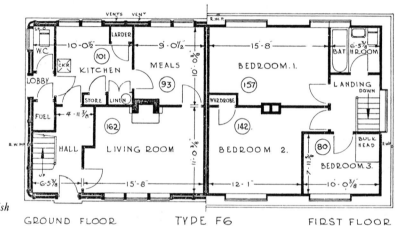

GROUND FLOOR   TYPE F6   FIRST FLOOR

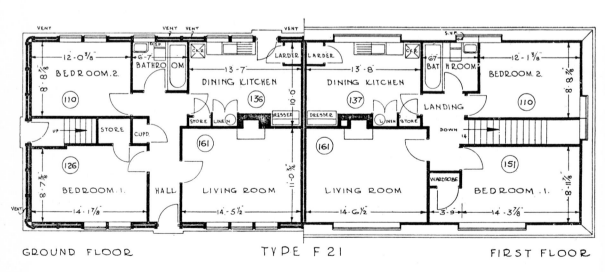

GROUND FLOOR   TYPE F 21   FIRST FLOOR

Minister of Health, and his enthusiasm for them was largely instrumental in securing approval for the design to be included in local authority housing programmes. Standard plans and specifications were drawn up and the first building programme, started in September 1946, included two kings of bungalow and several different types of house. More than 40,000 dwellings were built by this system between 1946 and 1956. They were the first really satisfactory concrete houses to be made in Britain, and, although they are no longer used in local authority schemes, there is a ready demand from private purchasers. Subsequent designs have tended to use more plasterboard and less concrete in the internal construction and there have been considerable variations in the type of wall-cladding. Concrete panels made of Reformite, which uses a china-clay waste-sand aggregate, have a pleasant texture and have met with above-average approval.

The Cornish Unit house was planned and first constructed at a time when wartime shortages had caused the Government and, through its influence, local authorities to experiment to a degree which would have been extremely unlikely under normal peacetime conditions. Two other types of factory-built experimental house were produced for local authorities in large numbers during the same period. The first type had a roof and outer skin of asbestos-cement sheeting, the second of aluminium alloy. Both were originally intended to have a maximum life of only ten years, but with the housing shortage persisting apparently indefinitely, many of these 'temporary' houses are still occupied more than a quarter of a century since they were erected. Neither type of house was particularly elegant, and the popular name for them, 'pre-fabs', did not indicate a very high level of public regard. They were, however, a good deal more comfortable, convenient and labour-saving than many of the 'permanent' council houses and flats

The developed Cornish Unit house

built subsequently. They contained a number of innovations – central, one-piece units for heating and plumbing and fibre-glass insulation – which were to become standard practice in later housing projects. The aluminium bungalows and houses were particularly interesting. After the war, both the aircraft and aluminium industries had surplus production capacity and housing seemed one obvious answer. Between 1945 and 1948 78,000 aluminium bungalows were built. Most of them used aircraft scrap, which was in plentiful supply at the time. Each bungalow contained about $1\frac{3}{4}$ tons of aluminium. It was used in two forms, extruded sections and clad-sheet, aluminium alloy which is further protected against corrosion by being given a coating of the pure metal. The box-sectioned wall frames were filled with foamed concrete, faced internally with plasterboard. The ceilings were made of fibre-board.

Aluminium, even scrap-aluminium, is an expensive material and for this reason the designer has to use the minimum quantity that will give the strength required. Aircraft designers were, of course, used to approaching problems in this way, because, quite apart from the problem of cost, the need to save every possible ounce of weight is extremely important in aeronautical engineering. The aluminium bungalows consequently had the benefit of extremely sophisticated production techniques. It is not, unfortunately, easy to study examples of aluminium houses, since most of them have now been demolished. A small group survives, however, at Hucclecote, on the outskirts of Gloucester, very close to the factory, now ICI Fibres, where many of them were built.

To make a complete house out of aluminium was something quite new, although the building industry had begun to think seriously about aluminium in the early 1930s, when the extrusion process, which had been recently developed, allowed aluminium glazing bars to be produced at a price which made economic sense. Aluminium is well suited to the extrusion process, which makes it possible to produce complex shapes in a single operation. In addition to their efficiency – condensation and glazing channels can be included in the one extrusion – aluminium windows have the outstanding advantage of requiring no painting. In the 'thirties, when painting costs were low, this was of only marginal importance, but nowadays it is a major factor in deciding which kind of window frame to install. Before the Second World War, one found very few aluminium frames in houses. The main customers were commercial and public institutions, which had the money to engage forward-looking architects and which could place a large enough order with the manufacturers to get the made-to-measure job they required. One of the earliest buildings in Britain to have aluminium window and door frames was the Friends' Provident and Century Life prestigious new Bristol office in 1933. They are also to be found in the extensions to the Cambridge University Library and the Bodleian Library, both completed in 1939.

There was nothing new about metal windows as such. Factories and

Making use of redundant wartime aircraft factories and aluminium capacity – the aluminium bungalow, 1947. Assembly of kitchen units inside factory

Erection of aluminium bungalow on site

The aluminium bungalow on site and occupied. These bungalows were intended at the time to be temporary, and to have a maximum life of only ten years. Many however, still remain, although certain modifications have had to be carried out to make them still habitable, and up to modern standards

mills of all kinds and sizes had had them since the early nineteenth century, and they are still to be seen in many of these old buildings, often a trifle rusty, but still performing satisfactorily after more than 150 years. These cast-iron window frames were simply painted; they were not rust-proofed in any way. What became known as the galvanising process – dipping iron objects in a bath of zinc to give them a protective covering against rust – was available in the 1860s, but it was not at all widely used for house window frames until the 1920s, after casements had finally ousted the sash window. Even in the 1930s, however, the wooden casement was much more commonly found in new houses, partly because it was considerably cheaper and partly because iron window frames were associated with factories. In pre-war municipal flats, on the other hand, iron frames were a little more usual.

Of the other materials used in house building and which can fairly be called twentieth century products, one should mention especially the various forms of building board, plasterboard, asbestos-cement, fibre-glass and certain types of plastic, all of which have their archaeology, both at the site and at the factory.

The earliest kind of building board, introduced to the market under the names of pulpboard and millboard, was a British invention. The man chiefly responsible was D. M. Sutherland, who had carried out experiments in Edinburgh into methods of making boards from wood-waste. Sutherland established the Patent Millboard Company at

Sunbury-on-Thames in 1898. The company did well, especially in its exports to the United States, and the product was later improved to make a tougher, harder material, sold as fibreboard. This kind of board contains no resin as a bonding agent and it is unsuitable for conditions in which it is likely to become damp.

Since 1945, a different kind of board, technically known as particle board, has been available. It is made by chipping or shredding wood into very small pieces, mixing it with urea formaldehyde or one of the other synthetic resins and pressing it into sheets. The resin represents about 6% of the weight of the board. This important industry began as a means of making use of waste wood and has developed into a major branch of manufacturing, for which wood is specially grown. Particle board will tolerate moisture and has a much wider range of uses than pulpboard or fibreboard. Synthetic resins have also revolutionised the techniques of glueing wood and have consequently greatly extended the range of conditions under which it is possible to use plywood. The grade known as WBP – water and boil proof – plywood was developed during the war for aviation purposes. It uses phenolic resin glues. These WBP or exterior grade plywoods are much used as form-work or shuttering for concreting and one of the components of composite panels for inclusion in factory-built timber houses.

This is perhaps the best place to mention the essential difference between a pre-war – Second World War – and a post-war ceiling. Until 1939, most ceilings were made of plaster, applied to an under-ceiling of thin wooden laths nailed to the joists. Sometimes a wire-mesh was used instead of laths. A layer of coarse lime and sand plaster was applied first, with a thinner coat of harder gypsum plaster to provide a smooth surface. Cornices were usually bought by the yard, cut to length and fixed into place in the angle between the ceiling and the wall. The walls received a similar treatment.

During the war, the shortage of skilled plasterers, combined with the need to carry out rapid repairs after bomb-damage, made plasterboard and pulpboard ceilings normal. The method was and is to fix the boards to the joists, tape over the joints between the boards and give the whole area a thin skimming of gypsum plaster. When old houses have been demolished recently in areas subjected to bombing during the war years, it has been interesting to notice the two types of ceiling in the same house, the traditional all-plaster ones, which somehow stayed up, and the skimmed board type, which represented the repair.

Plasterboard is something of a misnomer. Plaster panels would be a more accurate description. It consists essentially of gypsum plaster sandwiched between two sheets of stout paper. Invented and patented in the United States in 1894, it was soon widely used in the United States, where it was welcomed because of a shortage of skilled plasterers. Trade union opposition delayed its acceptance in Britain until the 1920s, but during the 'thirties it was increasingly used by speculative builders as a substitute for lath and plaster. It was in good supply during the war and was in demand for repairing bomb-damaged premises and for lining huts. Plasterboard is a useful building material which, with a honeycomb core, makes excellent partition units. Its one serious defect continues to be that its sound insulating properties are poor, as many inhabitants of post-war flats have discovered. The poor heat insulation of the original type of plasterboard has been largely overcome by giving it a facing of aluminium foil on one side. The first time this foil-faced board was used in Britain was in 1949, when the Ministry of Works built 94 semi-detached and terraced houses in Canterbury for the War Office, as married quarters.

The dangers of asbestos have been revealed only recently. Until the 1970s, this fibrous mineral was universally regarded as a boon and a blessing to mankind, invaluable both for fire-proofing and as a building material. It was being spun and woven into fire-resistant fabrics as early as 1870. For some years the fibres which were too short for spinning were treated as a waste product and thrown away, but in 1900 an Austrian textile manufacturer successfully incorporated them in asbestos–cement sheets, using a continuous papermaking machine for the purpose. In 1911 British Fibro-Cement began production at Erith, in Kent, and in 1913 Turner Brothers, afterwards Turner and Newell, opened their asbestos–cement factory at Trafford Park, Manchester, to make roofing tiles. Corrugated Trafford Tiles were used for a number of important contracts in the early 1920s, including the roof of the Empire Stadium at Wembley. Turners are still at Trafford Park, with their identity concealed under the new name, TAC, which allows the range of products to be decently extended beyond asbestos cement.

Corrugated sheets of the size with which we are familiar today were first made in Britain in 1924, at a new TAC factory in Widnes. The first asbestos–cement pipes were made here in 1927. Water-pipes in this new material were approved by the Ministry of Health almost immediately. They were shown to have considerable advantages over iron; their resistance to corrosion is much superior and the jointing employed is flexible enough to absorb settlement or vibration without damage. Asbestos–cement sewer-pipes, first used in Britain in 1961, have had a similar success. So, too, have gutters and down-pipes, which are cheaper than their main rivals, iron and plastics.

Asbestos–cement products, like concrete, are heavy and bulky in proportion to their value, so that transport costs have to be watched very carefully. Because of this, manufacturing has not been centralised to any extent, except for those items like sheeting, which can be packed with little waste of space. For such products as water and sewer-pipes, the tendency has been towards local manufacturing wherever possible, and the factories are therefore mostly fairly small and well-distributed over the country.

It is possible, if not probable, that the use of asbestos–cement may already have passed its peak. The reason is partly medical, partly political. Much of the world's supply of asbestos has come from former colonial territories – the notable exception is Canada – where labour was cheap and relatively expendable. This inevitably had an influence on the price at which asbestos could be sold. It was a cheap material because it could be produced cheaply. With the ending of the colonial system and with growing awareness of the serious health risks to people working with asbestos, higher prices have to be paid for the raw material and expensive safety measures taken. At this point, asbestos begins to lose much of its commercial attraction, and it is more than a coincidence that the star of fibre-glass has been rising as the star of asbestos has been declining.

Glass-fibre or, as it used to be called, glass-silk, was made in Germany before the First World War. It remained a curiosity, however, until the late 1920s, when several countries, including the United States, began to take a more active interest in it. The real beginning of what is now a large and growing industry can be dated to 1930, when Chance Brothers embarked on the production of glass-silk at their Firhill, Glasgow, plant. It was sold under the trade name of Idaglass and was used mainly for insulation purposes. In 1938 Chance Brothers took a glass wool licence from the United States. To finance this, a joint Chance–Pilkington company, Glass Fibres Ltd, was formed. At the same time, a continuous filament plant was set up at Firhill. In 1948 all continuous filament production was moved to a new site in Glasgow, at Possilpark. A decision had already been taken to build a glass wool plant at Ravenhead, St Helen's, and Glass Fibres Ltd was reconstituted as Fibreglass Ltd, a wholly Pilkington-owned company. In 1958, the manufacture of glass-fibre reinforcements was moved from Possilpark to Valley Road, Birkenhead, and in 1971 to a purpose-built factory at Wrexham. The works at Possilpark and Valley Road were both closed down in 1971, and at that point the first stage in the development of the British glass-fibre industry can be said to have ended.

The manufacture of glass-fibre, either as a filament or as an insulating material, is very simple. Basically, it consists of melting sand, which means low raw material costs and high fuel bills. The processes are highly mechanised and the demand is increasing all the time. Glass-fibre is now the cheapest available insulating material for all types of construction, for shipbuilding, for factory and home insulation, and for electrical equipment. It is also extensively used for reinforcing plastics and concrete, with the enormous advantages of being light, strong, corrosion-proof and easy to cut and manipulate. Its greatest disadvantage is that, in its glass-wool form, it forms a bulky product largely composed of air, but this has been overcome by compressing it before packing.

Forty years ago, glass-fibre was unknown in the building industry. All the techniques of using it have had to be learnt in a single generation. It forms one of a group of new materials which could, imaginatively handled and planned for, bring about fundamental changes in construction methods, especially in housing.

Both the developed and the developing countries have serious housing problems and there are many well-informed people who believe that the solution must lie in a new type of building industry, based on industrial methods of production. The group of synthetic materials popularly known as plastics should be able to play an important part in this development. The market for plastics in house-construction is already considerable. In Germany it is the largest market of all and in Britain and the United States it is second only to packaging. So far, the main applications have been in the finishing sectors of the industry, the field of what builders call rainwater goods – gutterings and down-pipes – lavatory cisterns and seats, baths, floor-coverings, translucent roofing panels and door fittings. The possibilities for plastics in structures are still comparatively untested.

An increased use of plastics in building is likely to come partly as a result of improvements in organic polymers and partly as a result of combining plastics with other materials, notably glass-fibre. Fully supported plastic sheet could make a perfectly adequate roof covering and the time must be close when reinforced plastic will begin to be an acceptable substitute for structural timber. These developments will, of course, be met with determined opposition from both traditionalists and those with a vested interest in the old materials. Other things being equal, the matter will eventually be decided by price.

So far as the building industry is concerned, 1977 is a good time for stocktaking and forecasts, but a bad time for certainties. A large number of fundamental changes which should logically and theoretically already have taken place have not done so, possibly for political reasons, possibly because of conservatism, inertia and lack of imagination in high places. One sees this particularly clearly in the persistent failure to solve what is euphemistically known as 'the housing problem', which means, in blunt terms, either that large numbers of people have no separate home of their own at all or that far too many people are forced to live in an environment which is a disgrace to the twentieth century. One could put this another way by saying that almost every urban and suburban community represents the archaeology of failure, failure to control the greed and social irresponsibility of the developers and speculators. The majority of council estates are as miserable, mean, unsatisfying and simply inadequate as the majority of estates put up by speculative builders.

Industrial archaeologists whose chosen fields have been the eighteenth and nineteenth centuries have paid a good deal of attention to what has usually been described as 'workers' housing'. This ranges from the depressing, treeless, grassless acres of smoke-grimed terrace houses in the 'old' industrial areas – Manchester, Leeds, Birmingham, Newcastle and the rest – to the superior dwellings provided by 'enlightened' employers, such as Robert Owen and Sir Titus Salt.

Urban historians have tended to make similar distinctions, but their range of study has been wider, including the houses of the rich and the middle classes, as well as those of the labouring poor.

For the twentieth century, this approach seems entirely inadequate and inappropriate. The social pattern has become much more varied and fluid than that of the Victorian Two Englands (the England of the rich and the England of the poor), the living standards of the middle classes and the working classes have been merging to an extent which would at one time have seemed unthinkable, and the phrase 'workers' housing' no longer conveys any clear meaning. What we do have, however, and what is worth studying, is the evidence of what planners, architects and builders have done during the past three-quarters of a century to meet the growing demand for places to live. This, in single dwelling units and in whole areas, is the archaeology of housing. Some of these areas, it is true, are inhabited mainly by manual workers and weekly wage-earners and some mainly by the salaried middle classes. Some are much better to look at than others. Some have a reasonable ration of gardens, trees and grass verges, some have practically nothing of this kind. But all of them must presumably represent an attempt to obtain a return on capital, to produce housing which is saleable or lettable, and to work within the limitations and opportunities of contemporary materials, equipment and labour skills. The purpose of studying the archaeological evidence is to discover how and how effectively this was done.

All idealism is a reaction against the unsatisfactory nature of life as it appears to be at the moment. It is like this, it could and should be like this. If paternalistic industrialists such as Salt, Krupp and Pullman did nothing else when they planned more spacious, pleasant estates for their workers to live in, 'they dissociated the processes of industry from the idea of human degradation in a filthy environment; a useful dissociation', as the American sociologist, Lewis Mumford, has put it. [2] In Britain, Ebenezer Howard took this idea a stage further forward, by pointing out in his influential book, *Tomorrow*, published in 1898, that there was no solution within the boundaries of existing cities. One had to make new starts, by creating garden cities in the countryside. These would have a socially balanced population and an environment in which pleasant working conditions and pleasant living conditions were planned at the same time and interwoven. Howard's vision was formed and his book written before the major twentieth century agents of decentralisation – the electricity grid, the automobile, the telephone and the electronic mass media – had begun to make their impact. When the opportunity arose to put his ideas into practice, they were nearly always either misunderstood or debased. Only Letchworth and Welwyn, the first begun in 1903, with a density of only 12 houses to the acre, and the second in 1920, really established anything resembling the garden city as Howard conceived it. The garden city, a complete,

---

[2] *The Culture of Cities*, Secker & Warburg, 1945, p. 393.

functioning unit, was thought to be impracticable and too expensive; the dormitory suburb – the Garden Suburb was an earlier and superior version[3] – and the council estate replaced it as a truncated, debased, anaemic version of the original.

The fading of the dream can be documented all over Britain and by various kinds of houses. One can go, for instance, to twentieth century employers' housing, at Bournville, Port Sunlight or Street, and see how the solidly built houses of 1910 and 1920 with big gardens slip downwards, under the pressure of increased land values and soaring building costs, into the more fragile little suburban boxes with pocket handkerchief gardens of the post-1945 period. One can also visit, with great profit, England's first rural council houses, Fullfoot Terrace, completed at Montacute, Somerset, in 1912. They were made possible by the Liberal Government's Housing Act of 1909, which for the first time gave local authorities the power to build and let houses. The twelve houses at Montacute were built of the local Ham Hill stone. They were in two terraces and each had a large garden, three bedrooms, sewage, water and gas. The cost was £162 a house, which included the land, and the rent was 5s. 9d. a week.

Walking along Fullfoot Terrace now, one finds it difficult to believe that it was once considered entirely normal to construct working class houses to this standard and with so much land attached to them. It is true that some modernisation has had to be carried out in recent years, chiefly the installation of electricity and hot water and the conversion of one of the bedrooms to a bathroom, but most tenants of council

[3] Hampstead Garden Suburb was laid out from 1907 onwards.

houses built since 1945 would reckon themselves extremely lucky to be offered accommodation in Fullfoot Terrace, which was planned and completed in what one can only consider now to have been a golden period in municipal housing. It is significant that the next council houses in Montacute, built in 1921, cost six times as much and bear clear signs of the economies that had to be made in order to keep rents within a working class budget.

The problem of affordable rents was not, of course, peculiar to the rural areas. Throughout the 'twenties and 'thirties, there were a great many families, employed and unemployed, whose weekly income did not exceed 30s. To have £3 was to be prosperous. Overcrowding and undernourishment were widespread, and to the more enterprising planners and architects it was clear that the provision of new housing could not be considered in a vacuum, and that the problem could only be tackled effectively by planning housing and social services on an area basis and at the same time. Two examples, both from the 1930s, illustrate this.

Kensal House, at Ladbroke Grove in West London, was completed in 1936. It was financed and owned, very exceptionally, by the Gas Light and Coke Company, whose enormous gasworks was only a few yards away, across the Great Western Railway's main line. The site could hardly be described as idyllic, but on it were constructed what were claimed, probably correctly, to be the first genuinely labour-saving dwellings ever designed for working class families. There were 13 two-bedroom and 54 three-bedroom flats, in three blocks, 4 and 5 storeys high, grouped around gardens. They are still there and still occupied, refreshed recently by a coat of paint all over. The gasworks, however, has gone and from that point of view the area is no doubt rather more appealing than it was in the 'thirties. Kensal House provides an excellent opportunity to see what advanced housing for the working classes was like in the pre-war period.

A distinguished architect was chosen, E. Maxwell Fry. He worked closely and from the beginning with a sociologist and welfare expert, Elizabeth Denby. The aim was, in Fry's words, 'to build a group of homes where people whose incomes allow them little above sheer necessity could appreciate as full a life as can be'.[4] The tenants were nominated by Kensington Borough Council. They came from scheduled slum areas and many of them were really poor, that is, they had only between 3s. 6d. and 6s. a head left for food and clothing after they had paid rent and other essential outgoings.

The plan was for what was described as an 'urban village'. It included a nursery school and a clubhouse. There were internal staircases, since experience had shown that access from outside galleries was 'un-private, draughty, barrack like and loved by nobody'. The construction was, in the architect's description, 'of framed

The first results of the Lloyd George Act – pioneering council houses at Montacute, 1912. The houses are still in excellent condition, and the size and standard of construction make modern council houses appear very inferior

[4] *Flats: Municipal and Private Enterprise.* Published by Ascot Gas Water Heaters, 1938.

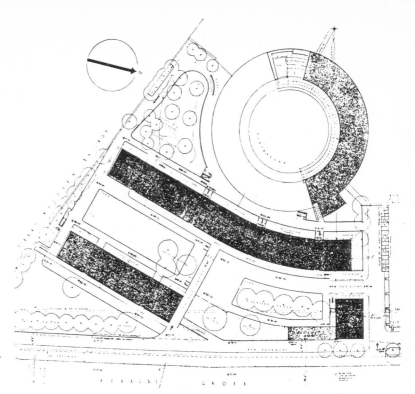

*Kensal House, Ladbroke Grove, London.
Site plan*

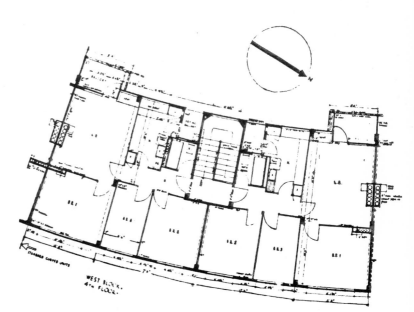

*Kensal House – plan showing room
arrangements*

Kensal House – view from the south-west, showing nursery school

reinforced concrete, with 4-in. walls lined internally with 1 in. compressed cork, and painted externally with concrete paint. Floors are of patent tile and concrete construction and are covered everywhere with battleship linoleum cemented to a floor screed.' Each flat had two balconies and a lock-up big enough to take a pram and a bicycle.

Kensal House was, not to put too fine a point on the matter, a working laboratory of gas equipment. There were Ascot water heaters to the bath, sink and copper, a gas cooker and gas lighting throughout. In addition, the coke fire in the sitting room was ignited by means of a built-in gas lighter, the main bedroom had a panel gas fire, the other bedrooms had points for portable gas radiators, and in the kitchen there was a point for a gas iron. This marked a complete break from the working class tradition of the combined kitchen-living room, with a solid-fuel range for heating and for part of the cooking, an establishment in which a woman could never shut housework out of her life. Of the 62 municipal housing estates built in London during the 'thirties, 84% continued this system of cooking in the living room, and 87% of them had no hot water system.

An enquiry carried out soon after Kensal House was completed showed that the weekly fuel bill in the average London working class household averaged about 6s. a week. At Kensal House, it was 4s. 6d.

Electric lighting would have added another 1s. to 1s. 6d. a week to the total. As will be pointed out in the next chapter, until 1945 electricity in Britain was very much a middle class amenity. The working classes could not afford it and, since coal and gas were cheap, they not unnaturally preferred to stay with these fuels.

An official of the Gas Light and Coke Company went so far as to say publicly that the electricity industry had no wish to provide all-electric houses for working class people, and would do a good deal to avoid getting it. 'They could not cope without upsetting their whole existing cost-structure and methods of charge, and without slowing down, or halting through increased prices the domestic progress of their industry. They need the coal range – the wizard of modernity must have at his elbow the smoky spirit of nineteenth century fuel.'[5]

In this respect, Kensal House should be put in the context of other working class housing constructed at the same time. Kennington Park Estate, built for the London County Council in 1936, had electric lighting and power points in the living room and bedrooms. So did the Rockingham Estate, Southwark (1936) and Vauxhall Gardens Estate (1935). Emily Street, Birmingham (1937–8) had power points and the model working class flats demonstrated at the Empire Exhibition, Glasgow, in 1938 had Belling electric cookers. Two points need making in this connexion. The first is that the provision of power points is no guarantee that they will be used and the second is that Kensal House was built for very poor people, at a time when the rents for new working class flats in London ranged from 9s. 6d. a week for two rooms to 17s. 6d. for five rooms. Middle class flats of the same period were being rented at £90–£150 a year. Against this background, Kensal House was a triumph of ingenuity, determination and clear thinking. It is beginning to look its age a little, but not disastrously so. After the war the Gas Company sold it to the Kensington Borough Council, which installed electricity, but in all other respects it is much as it was.

The equally publicised Quarry Hill Estate in Leeds is quite another story. Designed by the City Architect, R. A. H. Livett, in 1935, it ran into serious organisational problems, which overlapped the outbreak of war, and it was not completed and occupied until 1941. At the end of 1976, after years of vandalism and great changes in the surrounding area, the whole estate was finally abandoned as a hopeless proposition and demolished. It has to be sadly written off as one of the most tragic housing failures of all time and it cannot be studied now even as the archaeology of folly and misfortune.

It covered – one has to get accustomed to the past tense – 28 acres. There were 938 flats, in blocks ranging from 2 to 8 storeys, with the tallest blocks on the outside, giving the whole place much of the feeling of a medieval castle. There were shops, a day nursery, a communal

---

[5] Paper, *The Case for Gas*, by S. C. Leslie. Read at the B.C.G.A. Congress, Manchester, 1937.

Quarry Hill flats, Leeds, shortly before demolition

hall, a laundry, fitted kitchens, and a sink waste-disposal system. Even more pioneering and adventurous, there were 88 lifts. The Quarry Hill flats were, somewhat unbelievably, the only ones built by local councils during the 'twenties and 'thirties to have lifts. The working classes, it was officially believed, could not be trusted to operate lifts. All in all, Quarry Hill was reckoned to provide the finest working class accommodation in Europe.

In an attempt to keep construction costs down and so to pay for the unusual amenities, the architect chose the French Moplin system, the most completely pre-fabricated system available at the time. The system appeared to have worked well in France, but in Leeds it was a disaster. The factory production of the vibrated concrete units was never properly co-ordinated with erection and finishing on the site and the amount and type of skill required to handle and fix the slabs had not been appreciated. The contract dragged on and on and all the hoped-for savings were lost.

Much worse was the fact that the families re-housed from the Leeds slums hated Quarry Hill from the beginning. They had no wish to live in flats at all and regarded what they were offered as temporary, until they could find what they considered a proper home. Successive waves of tenants came more and more from the feckless and irresponsible levels of society and Quarry Hill degenerated into a giant and eventually uninhabitable slum.

Councils, and especially what was now the Greater London Council, made the same kind of blunder during the 'fifties and 'sixties with the building of high-rise flats. These were designed, not because the tenants wanted to live this way, but because they represented fashionable architectural thinking and because there was great pressure from the major construction firms, anxious to push their new methods of systems-building and pre-fabrication. The human scale of Howard's horizontal garden city was abandoned in favour of what was claimed to be something more in accordance with modern needs and conditions, vertical garden-cities, with green spaces and trees between the blocks. Only in this way, the public and the Ministry were told, could the horrors of urban and suburban sprawl be prevented. Once again, it was assumed that tenants would grow to like the new way of living, once they had experienced it, the never-expressed hint being that if they did not like it, they had better learn to put up with it, because this was all they were going to get. In the peak year, 1965, 10.6% of all local authority dwellings for which tenders were approved were in blocks of 15 storeys and over. By 1970 it had dropped back to 1.8%, the fall being assisted, but not caused, by the spectacular collapse, after a gas explosion, of one corner of Ronan Point, a 22-storey block in the London borough of Newham.

In 1970 a survey carried out by the Ministry of Housing and Local Government[6] among families living on high-rise estates in Leeds, Oldham, Liverpool and London showed that nearly three-quarters of those living in multi-storey flats would have preferred to be in a house. The reasons are those that might have been expected – because they wanted a garden, because it would be better for the children, and because it would provide more privacy and less noise. There were frequent complaints about refuse disposal, difficulties of cleaning windows, drying washing, damp, condensation, communal stairways and the condition of the lifts. Anyone who has lived in such blocks will know exactly what is meant. In our efforts to abolish old slums, we have, with the best of intentions, created new and in some ways worse ones. It is a bitter comment on three-quarters of a century of new materials, new methods, new social concern and on public financing on an unprecedented scale. With all the brains and incentive at our disposal, we have so far accomplished little better, so far as urban working class housing is concerned, than the dreariness of vast estates of terraces and semi-detacheds and the squalor and discomfort of multi-storey blocks. It may well be that only a declining population will allow us to do better.

That the public has been the victim of a series of confidence tricks there can be no doubt. For political, commercial and professional reasons, everything has been portrayed as far better than it really was and is. Skilful photography can accomplish a great deal to grade up housing and the photographs are always taken and the awards made

Housing that tried to demolish itself – Ronan Point, 1973, after a gas explosion in one of the flats. High-rise housing became noticeably less popular after this incident

[6] *Families Living at High Density.* HMSO, 1970.

when the estates and blocks are brand-new, and before vandalism and dilapidation has occurred. A highly important task for the archaeologist is to survey twentieth century housing as it really is, with its failings and blemishes as well as its good points, and to relate it to the professed aims of those who designed and built it, and to the ambitions and living styles of those who have had to inhabit it. This, after all, is exactly what industrial archaeologists have already done for nineteenth century housing. There is no reason why the twentieth century should not be served in the same way. If archaeologists fail to carry out the task objectively, other people are all too likely to do so for political and less disinterested motives.

six Shelter: domestic equipment

An interesting museum experiment would be to reconstruct two semi-detached houses, one of 1900 and the other of the type built today, side by side. Each would have all the furnishings, fittings and equipment of the period and visitors would be able to compare the housewife's tasks and tools in a way which might well cause considerable surprises. What would be immediately noticeable would be the vast amount of hand labour required at the earlier date. Cleaning, washing, cooking and heating all demanded human energy. Stoves and cookers had to be black-leaded, floors and tables scrubbed, coal carried, grates cleaned out and fires lit. Pots and pans had to be boiled with soda and scoured with steel wool. There were no stainless knives; what there were had to be cleaned and sharpened frequently to keep them in serviceable condition. In exceptionally well-to-do homes, hot water for the kitchen and bathroom was available from gas geysers, but elsewhere it had to be heated up specially in pans, cauldrons and saucepans on the coal range. Clothes were washed in large boilers known, whatever metal they were lined with, as coppers, underneath which a fire had to be lit on wash-day. Bars of soap were shredded and put into the washing water. Hand-operated wringers were available to squeeze the water out of the washing and ironing was carried out with heavy flat-irons, which had to be heated over a fire. Dust was not removed from a room; it was moved from one place to another by means of brooms and pieces of cloth known as dusters. Food had to be chopped and minced and mixed by means of sharp knives, whisks and hand-operated mills. Lighting was almost universally by gas in urban households and by oil-lamps in the countryside. The only mechanical items to be found at all frequently, apart from clocks and mangles, were sewing machines, available from the late 1850s, and carpet-sweepers, patented in America by Melville R. Bissell in 1878.

All this adds up to households with a great deal of overworked woman-power and no horse-power. The revolution – again, the word is certainly not too strong – which has taken place during the twentieth century has occurred in two fields. The first has consisted of giving the housewife powered equipment and the second of developing and making commercially available a wide range of new labour-saving materials. The two together have transformed housework and the

SEWING MACHINES AND ACCESSORIES.

WILCOX & GIBBS' AUTOMATIC CHAIN STITCH MACHINE. (Foreign).

Price, Complete with Stained Box £3 0 6
Rebuilt Machines as above can also be supplied 7 7 6
Or, complete with Treadle Stand with No. 4 table, cover and drawer in Walnut 7 15 0

THE "EMPRESS."

"Empress" Hand-machine. (British made.) With **Rexine Cover** and all useful attachments. Base measures, 14½ × 9 ins. Exceptional Value **£4 3 6**

THE "ANCOS" HAND SEWING MACHINE.
(As illustration.)

British-made throughout. All the Latest Improvements. This is a high-class Lockstitch Machine manufactured expressly for the Society. Fitted with all the latest improvements: High Arm, Self-setting Needle, Tension Releaser, Plated Wheel; also Reverse Feed; silent, simple, light running and beautifully finished. Complete with wooden cover £5 10 0

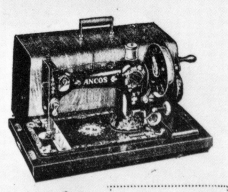

Any of these Sewing Machines can be supplied with a small but very effective electric motor which can be run from the nearest electric lamp holder. Complete with needle light.
Price £4 2 6

THE "JONES" CABINET SEWING MACHINE.

This Cabinet, both in finish and quality, is a piece of high-class furniture. It can be supplied in oak or walnut. The driving wheel works on ball-bearings and ensures light and easy running. This Cabinet can be fitted with Medium Cylinder Shuttle or Central Bobbin. £18 0 0

British-made throughout. Shown open and ready for working. The top thus forms a good table, affording ample room to work in comfort.

JONES' FAMILY HAND MACHINE
With Walnut base and cover. (British made.)

Reverse feed will sew backwards or forwards at will **£6 6 0**
Complete with Accessories and Instruction Book.
Central Bobbin Hand Machine **£8 16 0**

FRISTER & ROSSMAN'S HAND SEWING MACHINE.
(Foreign.)
This Machine makes a perfect stitch on either thin or thick material with the same appearance on both sides.

No. 50 Reversible Feed Complete **£6 16 6**
Cabinet Machine in Walnut 16 16 0
Latest Model Hand Machine, with Central Bobbin 7 19 6
All Machines are supplied Complete with Set of Attachments.

SEWING MACHINE ACCESSORIES.

Wilcox & Gibbs' Automatic Machine Needles	.. per doz.	2 3	**Wilcox & Gibbs'** Oil .. per bot.	-/8
Jones' Machine Needles	.. "	1 6	Short Straps for Hand Machines each	-/9
V.S. Machine Needles	.. "	1 6	Long Strap for Treadle Machines	1/-
Army and Navy Oil	.. per bot.	-/8	Shuttles, Vibrating Shuttle .. each from	3 6
			Shuttles (Old Style) .. "	3 6

When ordering needles customers are requested to send a pattern.
ALL EXTRA ACCESSORIES AVAILABLE TO ORDER.

Sewing Machines of any make repaired.
ALL PRICES ARE SUBJECT TO MARKET FLUCTUATIONS.

appearance of houses out of all recognition, as a comparison between two so far imaginary museum houses would immediately reveal.

Before going on to examine these changes in detail, one should emphasise that, from a social point of view, the revolution has occurred very unevenly. Those with money have been able to have at least some of the new products many years earlier than those without money. This is partly, as the previous chapter has indicated, because the upper and middle classes in Britain had electricity in their homes long before the working classes did. When they first arrived on the market, most innovations were expensive and beyond the range of the mass of the people. It is of some significance to know that electric refrigerators were available in 1912 in the United States, but it is much more important, from the point of view of both the manufacturer and the consumer, to know how many people in Britain owned such equipment, in that or any other year.

A further consideration which has to be kept always in mind is that people will not necessarily want what is available and what they could theoretically afford to buy. If, for example, domestic servants are cheap and in plentiful supply, the servant-employing classes will not be greatly interested in labour-saving devices. This was the situation before 1914: it had ceased to be the situation by the 1920s. The 'twenties and 'thirties, therefore, were the years during which more and more middle class women had to get used to doing their own housework, a state of affairs which brought them as willing and even eager customers for labour-saving equipment. Since, during this period, it was the middle classes who already had electricity in their homes, sales of all kinds of electrical equipment were necessarily confined to them. The much larger and commercially more important working class market for such goods did not exist until the 1950s, when this section of the community had, for the first time, both electricity and money. At this point the working classes began to equip themselves with the hot-water systems, the vacuum cleaners, the washing-machines, the refrigerators and the food mixers which many, but by no means all, middle class households already possessed. Once this point had been reached – the Americans had got there many years earlier – the domestic equipment industry took off and manufacturing facilities could be established on a serious scale. This equipment was not confined to what was required for cooking and cleaning. As gardeners and handymen became steadily scarcer and more expensive, it became natural to replace their labours, too, by machines wherever this was possible, and to carry out one's gardening and household maintenance with the help of equipment driven by electric motors. Power-tools have been an important part of the twentieth century domestic revolution.

The statistics tell the story in an unmistakable way. The remarkable growth of domestic electricity consumption during the present century is evidenced by the following decade-by-decade figures:

The Army & Navy Stores was concerned with selling domestic equipment to the upper third of the British population. It is interesting to note therefore that at this date, 1939, the sewing machines in their catalogue were all woman-powered. In the middle of the advertisement however can be seen a small insert, a sign of the revolution to come, announcing that an electric motor was available as an extra amenity

	Domestic sales in GWH (Generated watts to the hour)	Domestic customers in thousands
1920	271	(all customers) 908
1930	1,401	(1932) 3,989
1940	5,632	8,456
1950	13,794	10,567
1960	31,636	13,931
1970	66,134	16,435
1975–6	75,063	17,474

In 1948 40% of British households had vacuum cleaners; by 1963 the figure had risen to 72%. The increase in the ownership of washing machines, 4% to 50%, and of refrigerators, 2% to 33%, was even more impressive. Over half a century, from 1921 to 1971, the percentage of British homes with an electricity supply rose from 12 to 97, and a large proportion of this increase took place during the 1950s and 1960s. Such figures, however, tell only part of the story. The cost of electricity at different periods is also important. Until well into the present century, electricity was both expensive and unreliable. In the 1880s, a unit of electricity cost 6d. in those parts of London where a supply was available. In terms of today's money, this would be about 50p. There was therefore no question of using electricity for heating, since both coal and gas were cheap. All-purpose electricity, at a price which made it attractive to those with middle class incomes, did not come until the 1930s, by which time the Central Electricity Board had co-ordinated and rationalised the activities of nearly 600 separate local undertakings. The middle classes began to buy their electric fires, cookers, irons and immersion heaters during this period. The working classes had to wait another 20 years for the privilege, and 20 years after that the short-lived age of cheap electricity had gone, possibly for ever. Much of the heat-producing equipment installed during the 'fifties and the 'sixties, storage and under-floor heating in particular, now costs more to run than many of its owners can afford, which is why an increasing proportion of houses and flats are damp and suffer from condensation problems.

Against this background, which one might perhaps call the social history of electricity, one can list the first arrival of the main technical developments within the electrical industry which, over what is now getting on for a century, have transformed the British home and greatly reduced the physical burden of household tasks. Whether this has resulted in greater contentment and whether the time and energy saved have been used for more worthwhile purposes is beyond the scope or intention of the present book.

1880   Sir Joseph Swan's house, at 99 Kells Lane, Low Fell, Gateshead, was illuminated by incandescent lamps, the first house in Britain to be lit in this way.

1881   Many public installations of incandescent lamps were put into service, one of the most extensive being at the Savoy Theatre, London.

1882   Brighton power station opened, providing the first permanent and commercially viable public electricity supply in Britain.

1889   An electric fan marketed by the Westinghouse Co. of America, the first of the commercially manufactured small power units to be used in the home.

1890   The British General Electric Company's catalogue showed it was now selling electric irons, fans, immersion heaters, and an 'electric rapid cooking apparatus, which boiled a pint of water in twelve minutes'.

1891   Electric cookers demonstrated at the Electrical Exhibition at the Crystal Palace.

1907   Electric washing-machines first marketed in the United States (1917 in Britain).

1908   Vacuum cleaners available in the United States, under the name of 'electric suction sweepers'.

1912   Electric refrigerators introduced in the United States (1918 in Britain).

1929   Work begins on the construction of the National Grid (completed in 1934).

1948   The British Electricity Authority and the 14 Area Electricity Boards became responsible for the public supply of electricity.

1954   Electric floor-heating, an experiment by the South-East Scotland Electricity Board and Kirkcaldy Corporation in an 8-storey block of municipal flats.

1961   First marketing of domestic storage radiators.

The present size of the industry concerned with manufacturing electrical appliances in Britain makes its difficult to realise how small the scale of operations was before the Second World War. In 1939 a total of 970,000 domestic cookers were sold, of which 220,000, or 23%, were electric. In 1950, before the post-war boom really got under way, the total was 1,090,000, of which 275,000, or 25% were electric. By 1970 the proportion had risen to 35%. These figures should be interpreted with caution, because during the 1950s many of the gas cookers sold were certainly for replacement, whereas a higher proportion of electric cookers were probably for first-time buyers. But, whether one cooks by gas or electricity, to possess a cooker is not necessarily the same as to use it and, although no satisfactory research has yet been carried out into the matter, it may well be that the steadily

Early electric cookers, as displayed in the Domestic Appliances Gallery, The Science Museum, London

increasing popularity of snacks and convenience foods means that the average cooker is in use for a shorter time each day, compared with 20 or 30 years ago, and that the kettle works relatively harder than any other item of electric kitchen equipment. The enormous growth in the sales of synthetic fabrics must have brought about another important change, in that less ironing is done nowadays.

The development during the past 100 years of the kind of kitchen equipment we have been discussing can be followed in the interesting, but scandalously inadequately housed Domestic Equipment Gallery in the bowels of the Science Museum in London. There is, alas, no catalogue or handbook to accompany and explain the collection, so that its impact is not as great as it might have been. In particular, there is no information at all, apart from bare names, concerning the firms which made these early washing machines, water heaters and vacuum cleaners, or about the places where they were in business. Some details of this may therefore be helpful here, especially since the mergers and takeovers of the past 30 years or so have created within the industry a new pattern which has obliterated many of the once familiar names and landmarks and brought others into being in the process. The key dates in this long process of merger and re-combination are:

1881   The Edison and Swan Electric Light Company formed in Britain to make Ediswan lamps.

1889   The General Electric Company established in Britain, completely independently of the American GEC.

1894   British Thompson Houston (BTH) set up, as a subsidiary of the American GEC, to make electric lamps. It began to use the trade name, Mazda, in 1911.

1899   British Westinghouse formed, building a large factory at Trafford Park, Manchester.

1918   British Westinghouse merged with the electrical interests of Vickers and the Metropolitan Carriage works to become Metropolitan Vickers.

1919   Creation of English Electric, from a hotch-potch of companies making light electrical goods. English Electric buys Marconi in 1947 and Elliott Automation in 1967.

1929   BTH merges with Metropolitan Vickers to form AEI.

1967   General Electric buys AEI.

1968   General Electric buys English Electric.

Before one can look at what there is in the way of manufacturing archaeology, it does no harm to try to get one's bearings.

There are two major archaeological complications. The first is that, for many years, most of the refrigerators, washing machines and vacuum cleaners sold in Britain were in fact manufactured in the

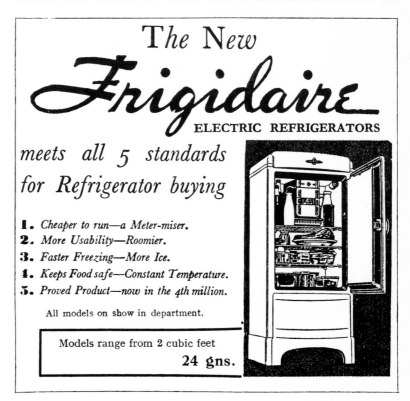

The New

Frigidaire

ELECTRIC REFRIGERATORS

meets all 5 standards
for Refrigerator buying

1. *Cheaper to run—a Meter-miser.*
2. *More Usability—Roomier.*
3. *Faster Freezing—More Ice.*
4. *Keeps Food safe—Constant Temperature.*
5. *Proved Product—now in the 4th million.*

All models on show in department.

Models range from 2 cubic feet
24 gns.

Refrigerators in 1939–40

135

Vacuum cleaners in 1939–40

United States, so that the early factories connected with these particular branches of the industry are to be found, where they have survived at all, on the other side of the Atlantic. The second difficulty facing the industrial archaeologist who wishes to work in this field is that, right up to the First World War, the market was so small that much of the equipment was made in workshops, rather than factories. Very little is known about these workshops, since a great deal of the work was carried out on sub-contracts. The story of the General Electric Company illustrates this.

What is now Britain's biggest concern in electrical manufacturing had its origins in the General Electric Apparatus Co., set up in 1886 in a City of London warehouse – now gone – by Hugo Hirst, who afterwards became Lord Hirst of Witton. Hirst's company made nothing at all to begin with, commissioning small workshops to make whatever was required, as the orders came in. By 1890, having changed its name to the General Electric Company, it was offering to provide every type of apparatus at that time available – irons, fans, kettles and immersion heaters – and it was manufacturing on its own account in Birmingham, in a factory at Witton, a place name which Hirst subsequently added to his title. The General Electric Company still has a manufacturing plant at Witton. Birmingham was also the home of Premier Electric Heaters, which pioneered this type of equipment in Britain and set up its first factory in 1907. Another well-known manufacturer of electric fires, Belling and Co., began manufacturing at Edmonton, in North London, in 1912.

The Hoover Company began making its vacuum cleaners in America in 1908. Eleven years later, in 1919, Hoover Ltd was set up in London to market the firm's products in Britain. The English Electric Company was formed in 1919, but it did not venture into the domestic appliance field until 1927, when it began to mass-produce cookers, electric fires (of the once popular but now obsolete 'bowl' type) and electric irons. Electrolux, another famous pre-war name in Britain, began making its vacuum cleaners and refrigerators here in 1927, instead of importing them from Sweden, as it had done up to that time.

Most people would consider gramophones, radios and television sets to be part of their household equipment, although, like cameras and hair-dryers, they can hardly be ranked as necessities. It is very difficult to decide what should and should not be brought under the broad heading of 'shelter'. Shelter is certainly something more than what remains after the removals men have cleared the house and loaded their vans. The modern house or flat in all its rooms is a much more complex, although not necessarily more cluttered living and working area than anyone could have imagined even as recently as 1900. The telephone is presumably to be considered a method of linking up the home to a general communications network and the moving men certainly do not take it away with the chairs and the tables. It is, in that sense, indisputably part of the home and of what one is calling here shelter. But a radio or television set, too, is part of a communications network. They may provide entertainment as well as information, but the same could be said of the telephone. The central point of the argument is that during the twentieth century ways have been found of bringing the world into the home, whereas previously one had to leave the home in order to hear and see the world. In defining 'shelter', it consequently seems illogical and churlish to ignore those innovations which have been instrumental in making the home a more self-contained unit. They will not be ignored here. It is not, perhaps, sufficiently realised, however, by those who have been brought up to take these items for granted that for many years after their first introduction they were all great luxuries, to be found only in the homes of the middle class and of exceptionally well-paid artisans. Up to the First World War new gramophones were sold almost entirely to a middle-class market. They cost at least £25, which was an impossible figure for anyone whose wages were only 30s. or at the most £2 a week, especially since the gramophone was no use without the records and a 10-inch record cost more than two dozen eggs. The social basis of the gramophone industry certainly widened considerably during the 'twenties and 'thirties, but the truly mass market only existed from the late 'forties onwards.

Archaeologically, the development of the gramophone industry in Britain is unusually well documented. The original London headquarters of The Gramophone Company,[1] later to become EMI, is still in existence at 31 Maiden Lane. The first recordings were made in the basement of this building. The task of making the pressings from these master-recordings was carried out by the Company's German subsidiary. In 1902 a move was made to 21 City Road, which is also still there, and which continued to provide all the studio accommodation required until 1930, when new studios were built at 3 Abbey Road, St John's Wood. The studios were completely modernised in 1971, but the house in front, which forms the office and reception area, is much as it was. From 1907, pressings were made at a large new factory at Hayes. In 1971 this was converted to other purposes and a second and much bigger factory opened in Uxbridge Road nearby.

The other major gramophone company operating in Britain, Columbia, was founded in the United States by Thomas Edison. In 1906 Columbia bought a factory in Garrett Lane, Wandsworth, with a sales and distribution centre in Worship Lane in the City. In 1911 it moved to 102–8 Clerkenwell Road, which can still be seen. The recording studios were located, for quietness and freedom from vibration, on the fifth floor and, since the lift went only to the fourth, even the most distinguished and portly artists had stairs to climb.

When electric recording became available in the late 'twenties, Clerkenwell Road proved to be no longer suitable for recording,

---

[1] Popularly known as His Master's Voice, or HMV, from the dog who figured on the company's trade mark.

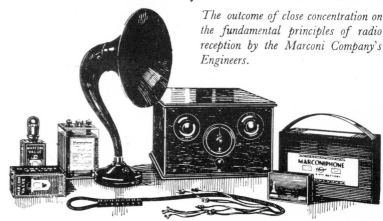

The 1928 radio

because of interference from the trams which ran along the road below the studio. A studio specially designed for electric recording was therefore set up in Petty France, Westminster. It continued in operation until Columbia merged with The Gramophone Company in 1931. At that point, recording was transferred to St John's Wood and pressings from Wandsworth to Hayes.

There are consequently at least ten sites belonging to the manufacturing history of the British gramophone industry which can still be visited, a very exceptional state of affairs. One should not, however, forget the selling side. Until the 1920s, gramophones and records were not, for the most part, sold under particularly good conditions. The Gramophone Company then decided to embark on a campaign to improve the industry's image, especially in wealthy and influential circles. It bought 363 Oxford Street and remodelled it, in its manager's words, with 'Sheraton style fittings and large, well-furnished rooms, to impress the trade and to bring the gramophone on to a higher plane than was suggested by the second floor of a piano showroom or an ironmonger's premises.'[2] Oxford Street was not, of course, Britain, but in those days it served an élite trade, with which it was useful for a company to be associated. The staff, 'not the ordinary run of shop assistants, but mostly young ladies of good families', stayed for years, guiding wealthy customers through the new issues of classical music and putting on records for them to listen to.

By the mid-'thirties this world was rapidly disappearing. Oxford Street and Mayfair were no longer what they had been, and The Gramophone Company's showrooms were democratised. The Sheraton and the big, luxurious rooms went, to be replaced by smaller, much more basically furnished cubicles, where customers could listen to records unaided. Self-service, introduced from America in the early 'fifties, emphasised the revolution.

A history of radio and television is out of place here. All one needs to note as historical background is that the BBC began radio broadcasts in 1922 and a television service in 1937. In the early days of radio, a great many people made their own sets. The do-it-yourself side of radio has never been adequately recorded and certainly deserves a book to itself. For about ten years, it was a home industry to be compared with knitting or fretwork and with a large number of shops and manufacturers competing to supply the components. There was one important aspect of gramophones and radio, at least in their pioneering days, which made them particularly suitable for working class homes; neither of them required mains electricity and gramophones, indeed, required no electricity at all. Even if one bought a radio set readymade, the cost of a fairly simple piece of equipment could be very low. In 1928, a crystal receiver could be bought for 12/6

---

[2] Mr George Fenwick, in a communication to the author, May 12, 1977. Mr Fenwick, now in his eighties, was responsible for the Company's London shop-window for many years.

and a battery driven 2-valve set for £2 2s. Anything more elaborate cost between £20 and £30, although hire-purchase was readily available. The cash price of a 5-valve portable was £27 12s., or £5 down and 12 monthly payments of £2 4s. There is no doubt that by the early 'thirties the ownership of radio sets was not confined to the upper and middle classes. Figures issued by the BBC in 1932 showed a total of 4 million licence-holders, to which one had to add an unknown, but probably quite large number of what were officially known as 'pirate families', people who would not or could not pay the annual licence fee of 10s. The 4 million were very unevenly spread over the country, the ratio of licence holders to population being five times as high in London as in Scotland or Wales. There were, even so, an estimated 16 million people in Britain who listened to radio programmes in their homes in 1932, a total not reached by television until the mid-'sixties. Television's slow start was caused partly by the high cost of sets – more than £200 in the immediate post-war years – and partly by the poor regional coverage which existed for many years. A television set could not, in any case, be used without an electricity supply, until satisfactory portable receivers were developed by the Japanese in the late 'sixties.

Curiously enough, British manufacturers of radio sets were not greatly worried by foreign imports during the 'twenties and 'thirties. The problem was much more serious for other kinds of domestic appliances. British-made electrical goods benefited considerably when Britain went off the Gold Standard in 1931. Sterling fell by 30% against the dollar and American imports became much more expensive. The Import Duties Act of 1932 added a 20% duty on all imported electrical appliances and at that point even the most recalcitrant foreign firm found it advantageous to make its goods in this country, rather than to continue to export them from the home base. By 1935 only 3% of all the vacuum cleaners sold in Britain had been made abroad. Vacuum cleaners were, incidentally, much the best selling electrical line, sales doubling from 200,000 in 1930 to 400,000 in 1939. Most of these were sold on hire-purchase, for which the interest rates were very low during the 1930s.

The post-war electrification of Britain falls into two sections. On the one hand, there was the achievement of building major additions to the country's network of power lines, with the new power stations to provide the extra generating capacity required both by industry and for the greatly increased domestic consumption – by 1960 most homes in Britain had not only an electric light supply, but a power supply as well – and, on the other, there was an equally impressive expansion on the manufacturing side. Government policy was to spread industrial development outside the old industrial areas, and to encourage this firms were given the opportunity to acquire, on very favourable terms, war-time munition and armament factories. The electrical manufacturers played a prominent part in this process. GEC moved its domestic appliance division from Birmingham to Swinton, in

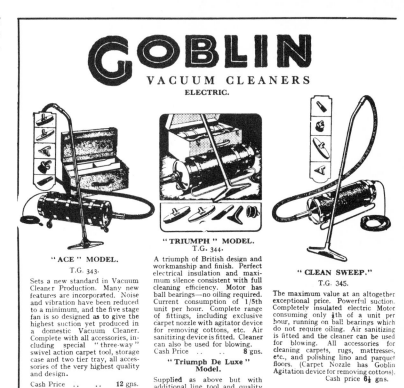

GOBLIN
VACUUM CLEANERS
ELECTRIC.

" ACE " MODEL.
T.G. 343.

Sets a new standard in Vacuum Cleaner Production. Many new features are incorporated. Noise and vibration have been reduced to a minimum, and the five stage fan is so designed as to give the highest suction yet produced in a domestic Vacuum Cleaner. Complete with all accessories, including special " three-way " swivel action carpet tool, storage case and two tier tray, all accessories of the very highest quality and design.

Cash Price .. .. **12 gns.**

" TRIUMPH " MODEL.
T.G. 344.

A triumph of British design and workmanship and finish. Perfect electrical insulation and maximum silence consistent with full cleaning efficiency. Motor has ball bearings—no oiling required. Current consumption of 1/5th unit per hour. Complete range of fittings, including exclusive carpet nozzle with agitator device for removing cottons, etc. Air sanitizing device is fitted. Cleaner can also be used for blowing.
Cash Price .. .. **8 gns.**

" Triumph De Luxe " Model.

Supplied as above but with additional line tool and quality storage case.
Cash Price .. .. **9 gns.**

" CLEAN SWEEP."
T.G. 345.

The maximum value at an altogether exceptional price. Powerful suction. Completely insulated electric Motor consuming only ⅓th of a unit per hour, running on ball bearings which do not require oiling. Air sanitizing is fitted and the cleaner can be used for blowing. All accessories for cleaning carpets, rugs, mattresses, etc., and polishing lino and parquet floors. (Carpet Nozzle has Goblin Agitation device for removing cottons).
Cash price **6½ gns.**

Yorkshire, and Simplex went from Birmingham to Blythe Bridge. The Pressed Steel Company began producing refrigerators in a former shell-making factory near its car-body plant at Cowley.

Other firms took advantage of the Government's policy of getting new industries established in areas where there were difficulties in providing sufficient employment. Hoover kept its headquarters and vacuum cleaner base at Perivale, in Middlesex, but opened two brand new factories, one at Cambusland, in the Scottish Development Area, and the other at Merthyr Tydfil, making washing machines, which were a new Hoover venture. Since then, a change of Hoover policy has closed its regional administrative and servicing centres, at such places as Birmingham, Bristol and Manchester, making Hoover archaeology more complex and, given the poor state of Hoover's archives, causing difficulties for historians in the future, when this important part of the twentieth century industrial story comes to be written with the perspective that only time can give. No attempt, incidentally, has been made to collect the reminiscences of a remarkable body of men, the Hoover salesmen of the 'twenties and 'thirties. Making their sales on a door-to-door basis and working almost entirely on commission, these men probably did more to make the British housewife conscious of the value of electric appliances than any other single category of person.

The post-war period has been enriched by the entry of several new

Lec Refrigeration, Bognor Regis. Assembly of domestic refrigerators, c. 1948.

'This new company has grown in 12 years from nothing to something very big indeed. The driving force all the way through has been Mr Charles Purley. Mr Purley came into engineering during the war and when the war ended he was looking for a field that really could benefit from energy and imagination. He found refrigerators fairly stagnant and ripe for attention. He was convinced that they could be made much more efficient and at a considerably lower price than had so far been accepted as normal. So he looked hard at every single detail of the design and the manufacturing process. The more you make yourself, the more you cut your costs, and this has been Mr Purley's first secret of success. Apart from the financial advantages, by having everything under your own roof you can make modifications quickly, without wasting time on specifications and quotations.

'I should like to quote something else that I was told at the factory. "One of the most important reasons for our success is that we haven't spent money on advertising. We've ploughed it back into development and equipment and that's helped us to keep the price down."' BBC radio news talk 26.5.59

firms into the industry. One of them, started by Kenneth Wood in 1947, was responsible for a mini-revolution on its own, when it launched the Kenwood range of toasters and food mixers and achieved an international success with them. Kenwood has since been bought up by the present giant in the British electrical appliance business, Thorn Electrical Industries. Until 1946 Thorn had concentrated on making lamps, very profitably. In that year, it went into the appliance market by buying an old-established company in the field, Tricity Electric; and it has since extended its empire by acquiring a number of other companies, some of which have been developed, some suppressed.

Two illustrations will show both the perils and the opportunities of electrical appliance manufacturing. The Lec Company, one of the leaders in the refrigeration industry, has succeeded in maintaining its independence. It had its beginnings in 1940, in a very modest workshop at North Bersted, on the outskirts of Bognor Regis, making small parts for defence contracts. In 1942 it moved into larger premises in Longford Road, Bognor Regis, and became registered as the Longford Engineering Company. By the end of the war, the decision had been taken to concentrate on designing and making refrigerators, in the belief that there was a huge pent-up demand for them. In 1946 a move was made to new buildings on the present Shripney Road site, at a time when the staff totalled 150. Longford Engineering Company became Lec in 1954, the company went public in 1964 and it has enjoyed almost uninterrupted success. Its factory site at Shripney Road now covers nearly 50 acres and the works employs 1400 people and produces more than 1500 refrigerators and freezers a day.

The other story has a less happy ending. Until three years ago, Dimplex could claim to be one of the great post-war success stories. Established in Southampton in 1947, it concentrated on oil-filled electric radiators, a brilliant idea, which made it possible to have something like central heating at a much lower cost. The radiators themselves were pressed out of sheet metal, a welcome departure from the traditional and much more bulky cast-iron radiator, they looked modern and pleasant, they took up little space and, in the golden days of what now seems ridiculously cheap electricity, they cost very little to run. As electricity prices rose, Dimplex descended slowly but inevitably into bankruptcy.

The lesson appears to be that, for space-heating purposes, electricity is far too expensive to use and that any company which has pinned its fortunes to this branch of the industry has inevitably been faced with declining sales. For every other kind of domestic electrical product the problem has been and continues to be that too many firms are in competition for a market which is not infinitely elastic and in which casualties are therefore unavoidable. Once the post-war boom was over, one saw this happening over the whole range of products, from radio and television sets to dishwashers, and from electric shavers to coffee percolators. This results in redundant factories, which in due course will be either demolished or converted to other purposes. The electrical appliance industry consequently has a rich and widely distributed archaeology, which is of four main types. There is first, and rarest, the small workshop and factory accommodation which was characteristic of the industry up to about 1914; the factories representing manufacturing in its first period of major growth, between 1914 and 1939; the new plants constructed during the 'forties, 'fifties and 'sixties; and fourth, the shops and showrooms which sold all these cookers, heaters, radio sets and the rest. One cannot, in the case of any consumer product, ignore either the retailing or the servicing side of the industry, and the system by which electrical goods have found their way from the manufacturer to the customer over a period of 70 or 80 years has never been properly studied. Suppose the date were 1925 and someone not living in London and not within easy reach of one of the major department stores was thinking of buying a vacuum cleaner or an electric kettle or cooker. Where would he or she go in order to see these things demonstrated or on sale? When one looks more closely into this problem, with the help of local directories and newspaper advertisements, it is possible to trace a most intricate and interesting pattern of development, containing the growth of the general electrical shop, which carried out wiring and installation in addition to selling lamps and lighting filaments and any kind of electrical equipment which customers might want; shops which sold radios, gramophones, bicycles and camping gear, jumbled together in extraordinary variety; ironmongers who added the simpler and cheaper kinds of electrical appliance to their traditional stock; from the 1930s onwards the showrooms run by the Electricity Boards themselves; and the electrical departments of the local department store, where such a place existed. To work out this pattern for a particular town, with the help of people with long memories of the district, is a worthwhile pursuit. It makes clear that before the Second World War the market for electrical appliances had an overwhelmingly middle class flavour to it. After the war, the chain shops, such as Curry's, and the cut-price stores began to dominate the market and a great many of the pre-war retailers went out of business. During this period, which one might

Encouraging the demonstrators. From Home Sales & Service *(a gas company publication), Vol. 4, No. 8, September 1938*

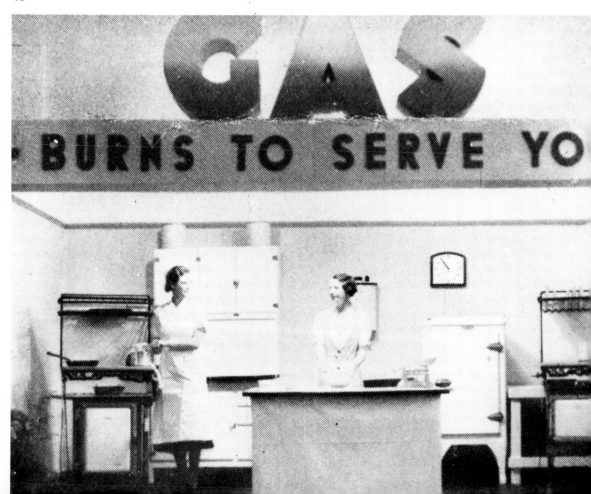

term the years of working class electrification, an increasing proportion of the goods sold have not been made in Britain at all, which, from a purely national point of view, makes the retailing history of these goods in many ways more interesting than their manufacturing history.

The gas story is simpler, partly because gas appliances were usually sold and installed by the individual gas companies themselves, not by independent firms, and partly because the range of such appliances has always been much smaller – cookers, radiators, water heaters, refrigerators and, more recently, central heating apparatus. But any study of either the gas showrooms or the electricity showrooms should take account of the very real contribution which both have made to public education. During the 1930s especially many new buildings were constructed to accommodate these showrooms and the local company offices. The practical cookery and housecraft demonstrations which were held there were an important factor in accustoming women to new equipment and to the techniques needed to get the best use from it, a process which has continued throughout the post-war period. These showrooms are an element within the archaeology of the power industries which should not be overlooked.

Cooking on coal ranges and, until the post-war period, on gas stoves was a somewhat crude business, demanding robust utensils which would stand up to regular exposure to naked flames. This meant, in practice, cast iron pots, saucepans and frying pans. For some purposes, such as heating milk or making sauces, the metal would be

"ECLIPSE" BRAND ALUMINIUM WARE.

"ECLIPSE" ELECTRIC COOKING UTENSILS have been scientifically designed to meet the peculiar needs of cooking by electricity.

A dead flat surface is given to the bottoms by special grinding processes, and an even $\frac{1}{4}''$ **thickness is obtained over the whole Machined bottom.** Thus absolute contact is given with the hotplate at every point minimising heat loss and the extra thickness retains the heat.

The handles are completely insulated and heat resisting, of patent reinforced Bakelite and have no screws to come off. There are no rubber washers (which so quickly wear out), and no wood to crack or warp.

The user of "Eclipse" Electric Utensils will find an immediate economy in electricity charges.

No. 457.
STEWPAN AND COVER.
Insulated Socketed Handle.
Polished Finish Throughout.

$4\frac{1}{2}$	$5\frac{1}{2}$	$6\frac{1}{4}$	7	8	$8\frac{3}{4}$	$9\frac{1}{2}$ ins. dia.
$1\frac{1}{2}$	$2\frac{1}{2}$	$3\frac{1}{2}$	5	7	9	12 pints.
8/9	9/9	10/6	12/9	17/3	20/9	24/- each.

No. 458.
PORRINGER.
Insulated Socketed Handles. Polished.

2	$3\frac{1}{4}$	5 pints.
15/-	17/-	20/6 each.

No. 460.
FRYPAN.
Insulated Socketed Handle.
Polished Finish Throughout.

7	8	$8\frac{3}{4}$	$9\frac{1}{2}$ in. dia. base.
$8\frac{1}{2}$	$9\frac{1}{4}$	$10\frac{1}{2}$	11 in. dia. top.
9/-	10/9	13/6	16/6 each.

No. 459.
KETTLE.
Brass Standards. Reeded Grip.
Polished.

2	3	4	7	10 pints.
12/6	15/3	19/3	23/3	30/- each.

No. 461.
STEAMER.
Black Insulated Side Handles.
Polished Finish Throughout.

7	8	$8\frac{3}{4}$ ins.
6/6	8/-	9/3 each.

enamelled, which was satisfactory until the enamel began to chip. The electric cooker, which produced no flame, introduced different possibilities. By comparison with coal and gas, electricity was an expensive source of heat and it consequently needed to be use. ... economically as possible. Intelligence, not always forthcoming, provided one answer to the problem, aluminium another. Aluminium is a very good conductor of heat, which means that food placed in aluminium containers cooks more quickly and with less consumption of energy. If the base of a pan is machined to a high degree of accuracy, the heat loss which takes place between the base and the heat source is greatly reduced. With aluminium, this kind of finish is easy to achieve. Aluminium pots and pans were available even before the First World War, but they were regarded with some suspicion, and very few households possessed them. Sales greatly increased during the 'twenties and 'thirties, largely as a result of intensive promotional campaigns, and nowadays there must be very few homes without them.

Aluminium, as a commercially viable material, dates from the 1890s. The British Aluminium Company was established in 1894 and set up its reduction works at Foyers, in Inverness-shire. A second works at Kinlochleven began operating in 1909. By 1911 the world output of aluminium was only 43,000 tons and, of this, 8000 tons came from Foyers and Kinlochleven. Having produced the metal, the problem was to find ways of using it. One possibility, from the beginning, was seen to be cooking utensils and one of the British Aluminium Company's publications issued in the late 1890s declared, somewhat optimistically, that 'heavy iron pans promise soon to be interesting relics of the past, and Cinderella downstairs, who wrenches her back lifting and carrying the clumsy iron stock pot, will certainly bless the fairy metal that alleviates her laborious task. . . .' This proved to be a little ahead of its time and, although some progress was made with popularising aluminium kitchenware during the first decade of the present century, the real advance came in the 1920s, when the great increase in productive capacity which had taken place during the war years made it essential to find peace-time uses for a metal which was now in more than abundant supply. Kettles and saucepans took up some of the slack. The situation was repeated after the Second World War, but on a much greater scale.

The first British manufacturing company to see the possibilities of aluminium for kitchen purposes were Brabys. They are still in business as the Braby Group. A catalogue produced by the company in 1925 says: 'We are the pioneer British makers of aluminium cooking utensils, which have stood 30 years wear. Our "Eclipse" and "Zephyr" brands are well known as a guarantee of excellence of quality.' Thirty years back from 1925 is 1895, so that Brabys must indeed have been very early in the field. They were originally sheet-metal workers and galvanisers, based at 352–364 Euston Road, London, with several factories in different parts of the country. One of

A page from an early 1920s Braby catalogue

147

these was at Coronation Road, Bristol, where the company was established in 1897. Coronation Road was soon outgrown, and a second and much larger Bristol works was built at Ashton Gate, where manufacturing is still carried out. The Ashton Gate works certainly included a section for making aluminium hollow-ware and Coronation Road may well have done, too. Perhaps the most significant point to notice about the history of Brabys is that, although they were one of the leading firms in the trade, the market for aluminium kitchen ware was not large enough to justify specialising in it, to the exclusion of other kinds of product. Galvanised sheet-metal was prudently regarded as the bread and butter line.

Since 1945 what can fairly be called the kitchen industry has transformed this part of the house out of all recognition. It has been converted from a mere workshop into a place where meals can be eaten in some elegance and without too obvious reminders of its main functions as a laundry, a food and drink store and the domestic equivalent of a ship's galley. The Victorian kitchen, much the most frequently found variety until well into the 1950s, was essentially a coal and iron kitchen, a hot, smelly place, a temple consecrated, like the Victorian household in general, to the Goddess of hard, unceasing manual work. The kitchen of the 1970s is an aluminium, electricity and plastics kitchen, kept in contact with the outside world by radio, telephone and often by television, a microcosm of the Second Industrial Revolution which has been taking place during the present century. It is the composite creation of a number of new industries which have grown up to provide it with its power-driven equipment, its special furniture and floor-coverings, its refrigeration and ventilation systems.

One of the most notorious sources of hard work in First Industrial

Revolution kitchens were the wooden surfaces of tables, draining boards and shelves. Once an easy-clean substitute had been found for wood, a great deal of the work disappeared. Stainless steel now looks after both the draining boards and the sinks they serve and plastic laminates have dealt very satisfactorily with the rest. This major new industry, which the housewife has reason to bless every hour of the day, was the creation of a single company, almost by accident. Formica, to call it by its trade name, was invented in Britain by the De La Rue Company in the mid-'thirties, as a side-line to the resin and paper laminates developed by the company for industrial purposes. To understand how and why this happened, one has to explain how De La Rue, who became internationally famous as playing-card manufacturers, came to be involved in plastics in the first place.

During the First World War, De La Rue were given control of a small German-owned factory in Shernhall Street, Walthamstow, which had been established to make products in a hard composition material. Between 1914 and 1918 this factory turned out millions of what were known as transit plugs for the Ministry of Munitions. After the war, this material was christened Telenduron and was moulded into a wide range of industrial components – lids for pickle jars, screw-tops for bottles and insulators for telephones were some of them. The business had been bought by De La Rue for a very small figure from the German owners. Its premises consisted of two adjoining houses with a shed in one of the gardens. Into these buildings were somehow crammed 150 people. Working conditions can hardly have been good and the fire hazard must have been appalling. The best customers were a father and son called Clark, who ran a small engineering business in Ilford, which they had bought from a man called Plessey,[3] whose name they decided to keep. The Plessey business made electrical appliances and bought their moulded insulations from De La Rue.

In 1926 De La Rue took what they felt was a great gamble and decided to expand the plastics side of their business, which was run quite separately from the printing and stationery sections. They bought a 10-acre site in Avenue Road, Walthamstow, and built a proper factory on it. Here they developed a different range of plastics, making their own moulding powders on the site, and gradually obtained contracts from Morris and Ford for window-frames and other car components, from Plessey, for Post Office telephone components – each telephone contained seven De La Rue mouldings, and for such humble domestic items as tooth-mugs, sold as Enduraware. A little later, they did very well out of moulded radio cabinets, especially for Ekco and Phillips.

By the early 1930s one part of the factory was producing an industrial laminate, made by bonding layers of paper with resin under great pressure. This was a first-class material for electrical insulation,

[3] Plesseys are still at Ilford. This very important company has wide interests in the electrical and electronic industries. The present Chairman, Sir Allen Clark, is the grandson of the founder.

but it was seen to have other potential applications. By laying wood-grained wallpaper on the top of the laminate and then bonding it in it was possible to produce sheets which could be used for decorative purposes. Mr Ernest Davis was the company's chief chemist at the time, and he recalls that his office adjoining the laboratory in Shernhall Street – the old premises had been kept on after the new factory was built – was panelled all round in 20-inch squares of this material. He has a kitchen table at home, with the top made from the same decorative laminate, known at that time as Delaron, and this may well be the earliest surviving example of it.

With the outbreak of war, decorative laminates were pushed into the background, together with tooth-mugs and radio cabinets. Wartime production at the Walthamstow factory was concerned with insulating laminates, plastic grenade cases, seats for aircraft cockpits and magnetic limpet bombs. After the war, De La Rue decided to get out of the manufacture of moulded plastics, which was showing strong signs of becoming an uncomfortably overcrowded trade, and to concentrate on decorative plastics. In order to do this more quickly, they bought the machinery and the goodwill of that part of the Metropolitan Vickers business at Trafford Park, Manchester, which had been making a decorative sheet, sold as Traffolyte.[4]

Faced with the impossible task of getting the necessary resin in the years immediately after the war, they also took a licence to use Formica sheet imported from the United States, since the Americans could get the melamine which was unobtainable in Britain. The situation was farcical, because De La Rue were being forced to buy know-how which they already had. Eventually, as the supply position improved, De La Rue made their own resins, keeping the Formica trademark.

The Trafford Park presses were moved to a new factory built by De La Rue at Tynemouth and from then on Formica was made in the North East. It was a good bargain. As Mr Davis recalls, 'We bought this whole outfit, two presses, impregnating machines, engraving machines, all the know-how. Two presses, one 4×4 and one 8×4, which we still operate, up in Tynemouth. I had the job of transferring the Metropolitan Vickers plant from Manchester to Tynemouth. It was in what was called the Transformer Department. They were terribly anxious to get rid of it; and to hold us over for a while we took an old cotton mill and put the impregnating machines in it.'

Without people like Ernest Davis, how would we know these things? And how, for that matter, would we still be able to see the decorative laminates, the early bowls, candlesticks, dressing table sets, trays and other objects in Enduraware, and the Metrovick sample-book of Traffolyte? The makers have kept nothing, the Science

[4] Traffolyte was sold as decorative panels for walls and as veneers for furniture. It was made in a number of grades, one of which was described as 'blister-proof', and especially suitable for table and counter tops. It had a sheet of aluminium foil just below the top surface. If a cigarette was laid on the table, the foil conducted the heat away, so that the plastic did not blister.

Museum has nothing, but Mr Davis has them all at his home in Essex, together with two products of one of the De La Rue subsidiaries, Thomas Potterton – a gas cooker called the De La Rue 'Warwick', and one of their gas boilers, the 'Diplomat'. Mr Davis's collection is no doubt exceptionally single-minded, but there must be few homes which are not in various degrees museums of twentieth century domestic appliances. The author certainly looks at his pair of superannuated Dimplex oil-filled electric radiators with a good deal of nostalgia, and at his storage heaters which also seem condemned, for reasons of expense, to become treasured museum-pieces.

What a conversation with someone of the calibre and veteran status of Ernest Davis also reveals is the remarkable interconnexions between pioneers in different branches of industry. Plessey interlocks with De La Rue, De La Rue interlocks with Ekco, Phillips and Morris Motors, Ercolani makes wooden radio cabinets, Pye buys him out for a million and a quarter and he gives up his factory next door to De La Rue in Walthamstow Avenue and puts the Pye money into building up the Ercol furniture company at High Wycombe. Industrial history can be very complicated, and many of the most significant facts are, unfortunately, never committed to print and only emerge in the course of conversations with people with first-hand knowledge of what took place.

Formica, however, is a wave which has already rolled over the head of De La Rue. In 1977 it sold its 60% holding in Formica International to the American Cyanamid Company, which already owned the remaining equity. Why did it do this? In order to re-invest the £9 million in an even more rapidly growing twentieth century industry, the security business. It is now, in other words, more profitable to protect other firms against dishonesty than to manufacture useful goods, a situation likely to provoke cynical thoughts.

But with Formica, as with any other new industrial product, one has to start with certain basic historical facts. Once one is armed with the name and address of the company concerned, one can see if the premises are still there and, if they are, how big they are, what their present use is, and whether they seem to have gone up or down in the world over the past 40 years. One can, in other words, take a careful look oneself, having previously acquired as much information as possible. The archaeology, the oral history and the documentary evidence can then be brought together into a single focus, which is the surest route one can have towards both an emotional and an intellectual understanding of the past.

The golden rule in industrial archaeology is that everything seems different, often very different, once one has taken a look at the place where the events took place. The scale is different, the proportions are different, the flavour is different, the significance is different. This is the whole point of industrial archaeology. It helps to sort out what is more important from what is less important. One has, very literally, one's feet on the ground.

Books for further reading

A. *General industrial, economic and technical development*

Ballin, H. H. *The Organisation of Electricity Supply in Great Britain* Electrical Press Limited, Maidenhead, 1946

Campbell, W. A. *The Chemical Industry* Longman, 1971

Davis, Dorothy *A History of Shopping* Routledge, 1966

Everard, S. *The History of the Gas Light and Coke Company* Bean, 1949

Habakkuk, H. J. *American and British Technology in the Nineteenth Century: the search for labour-saving inventions* Cambridge, 1962

Hardie, D. W. F. and Pratt, J. D. *History of the Modern British Chemical Industry* Pergamon, 1966

Heath, H. F. and Hetherington, A. L. *Industrial Research and Development in the United Kingdon* Faber, 1946

Hennessey, R. A. S. *The Electric Revolution* Oriel Press, 1972

Jefferys, James B. *Distribution of Consumer Goods* Cambridge, 1950

Jefferys, James B. *Retail Trading in Britain, 1850–1950* Cambridge, 1954

Matthias, P. *Retailing Revolution* Longman, 1967

Orwell, George *The Road to Wigan Pier* Gollancz, 1937

Pasdemadjian, H. *Management Research in Retailing* Heinemann, 1951

Plummer, A. *New British Industries in the Twentieth Century* Pitman, 1937

Pollard, Sidney *The Development of the British Economy, 1914–1967* 2nd ed., St Martin's Press, 1969

Rees, Goronowy *St. Michael: a History of Marks and Spencer* Weidenfeld and Nicolson, 1969

Richardson, H. W. *Economic Recovery in Britain, 1932–39* Weidenfeld and Nicolson, 1967

Richardson, H. W. 'The new industries between the wars', *Oxford Economic Papers*, new series, no. 3, 1961

Watton, E. B. *Holborn Viaduct to Calder Hall* Babcock and Wilcox, 1957

Wilson, C. H. *The History of Unilever* 3 vols. Cassell, 1954, 1968

B. *Food production, processing, retailing*

Beable, W. H. *Romance of Great Businesses* Vol. II. Heath Cranton, 1926 (for section on Spratts)

Beaver, Patrick *Yes! We have some: the story of Fyffes* Publications for Companies, 1976

Burnell, R. G. *Through the Mill: the Life of Joseph Rank* Epworth Press, 1945

Corina, Maurice *Pile it High, Sell it Cheap* The Authorised Biography of Sir John Cohen, Founder of Tesco. Weidenfeld and Nicolson, 1971

Corley, T. A. B. *Quaker Enterprise in Biscuits: Huntley and Palmer of Reading, 1822–1972* Hutchinson, 1972

Curtis-Bennett, N. *The Food of the People* Cassell, 1951

Davis, Alex *Package and Print* Faber, 1967

Drummond, J. C. and Wilbraham, A. *The Englishman's Food* Cape, 1939

Fraser, Colin *Harry Ferguson, Inventor and Pioneer* Murray, 1972

Gavin, Sir William *Ninety Years of Family Farming – the Story of Lord Rayleigh's and Strutt and Parker Farms* Hutchinson, 1967

Harvey, Nigel *A History of Farm Buildings in England and Wales* David and Charles, 1970

Jansson, Tage *The Development of Milking Machines: an Historical Review* Alfa Laval, 1973

J.S. 100: the Story of Sainsbury's J. Sainsbury Ltd, 1969

Keevil, Ambrose *The Story of Fitch Lovell* Phillimore, 1972

Packhouse – the Story of East Kent Packers East Kent Packers, 1970

Priestland, Gerald *Frying To-Night – the Saga of Fish and Chips* Gentry Books, 1972

Pudney, John *A Draught of Contentment* (history of the Courage Group) New English Library, 1971

Reader, W. J. *Birds Eye: the Early Years* Walton-on-Thames: Birds Eye Foods Ltd, 1963

Reader, W. J. *Metal Box: a History* Heinemann, 1976

Vaizey, J. *The Brewing Industry, 1886–1951* Pitman, 1960

Wainwright, David *Brooke Bond – a Hundred Years* Newman Neame, 1969

Waugh, Alec *The Lipton Story* Cassell, 1951

C. *Clothing: materials, manufacture*

Ashmore, Owen *The Industrial Archaeology of Lancashire* David and Charles, 1969

Beable, W. H. *Romance of Great Businesses* Vol. II (for section on Pullars of Perth) Heath Cranton, 1926

Coleman, D. C. *Courtaulds: an economic and social history* Oxford, 1969

Dobbs, S. P. *The Clothing Workers of Great Britain* Routledge, 1928

Hague, Douglas C. *The Economics of Man-Made Fibres* Duckworth, 1957

Hard, Arnold *The Story of Rayon and other Synthetic Textiles* Union Trade Press, 1939

Laver, James *Tastes and Fashion from the French Revolution to the Present Day* Harrap, 1945

Nixon, Frank *The Industrial Archaeology of Derbyshire* David and Charles, 1971

Ryott, David *John Barran's of Leeds, 1851–1951* Privately printed, 1951

Smith, David *Industrial Archaeology of the East Midlands* David and Charles, 1965

Stewart, Margaret and Hunter, Leslie *The Needle is Threaded* (history of the National Union of Tailors and Garment Workers) Heinemann/Newman Neame, 1964

Thomas, Joan 'A History of the Leeds Clothing Industry', *Yorkshire Bulletin of Economic and Social Research* Occasional Paper No. 1, 1955

Thompson, Francis *Harris Tweed – the Story of a Hebridean Industry* David and Charles, 1968

Wells, F. A. *Hollins and Viyella: a Study in Business History* David and Charles, 1968

Wray, Margaret *The Women's Outerwear Industry* Duckworth, 1957

D. *Building construction, housing, furniture, household equipment*

Bloom, John *It's No Sin to Make a Profit* W. H. Allen, 1971

Bowley, M. *Innovations in Building Materials* Duckworth, 1960

Braby Company *The Book of Braby Products* Privately printed, 1925

British Aluminium Company *The History of the British Aluminium Company Limited, 1894–1955* Privately printed, 1955

Brockman, H. A. N. *The British Architect in Industry, 1841–1940* Allen and Unwin, 1974

Burke, Gerald *Towns in the Making* Edward Arnold, 1971

Chapman, Stanley D. *The History of Working Class Housing* David and Charles, 1971

Cherry, Gordon E. *The Evolution of British Town Planning* Leonard Hill Books, 1974

Church, R. A. *Kenricks in Hardware – a family business* David and Charles, 1969

Collins, Peter *Concrete: the Vision of a New Architecture* Faber, 1959

Corley, T. A. B. *Domestic Electrical Appliances* Cape, 1966

Crawford, David (ed.) *A Decade of British Housing, 1863–1963* Architectural Press, 1975

Davey, N. *A History of Building Materials* Phoenix House, 1901

de Maré, Eric *New Ways of Building* 3rd ed. Architectural Press, 1958

Eyles, D. *Royal Doulton, 1815–1965* Hutchinson, 1965

The First Factory-Made Aluminium Bungalow Aluminium Federation, 1948

Flats: Municipal and Private Enterprise Ascot Gas Water Heaters, 1938

Houseman, Lorna *The House That Thomas Built: the Story of De La Rue* Chatto and Windus, 1968

Housing of the Working Classes, 1855–1912 London County Council, 1913

Hudson, Kenneth *Building Materials* Longman, 1972

The Market for Household Appliances Political and Economic Planning Council, 1945

Ministry of Housing and Local Government *Families Living at High Density: a study of estates in Leeds, Liverpool and London* HMSO, 1970

Ministry of Housing/Ministry of Works *Housing Manual 1944* HMSO, 1944

Pearson, M. *The Millionaire Mentality* (for information about Kenneth Wood and John Bloom) Secker and Warburg, 1961

The Principles of Modern Building HMSO, 1938

Ravetz, Alison *Model Estate: Planned Housing at Quarry Hill, Leeds* Croom Helm, 1974

Richardson, H. W. and Aldcroft, D. H. *Building in the British Economy between the Wars* Allen and Unwin, 1968

Sutcliffe, Anthony (ed.) *Multi-Storey Living: the British Working-Class Experience* Croom Helm, 1974

White, R. B. *Prefabrication: a History of its Development in Great Britain* HMSO, 1965

Whyte, Adam Gowans *The All Electric Age* Constable, 1922

Index